I AM
AN AMERICAN

I AM
AN AMERICAN

By Famous Naturalized Americans

★

Edited by
ROBERT SPIERS BENJAMIN

with an Introduction by
ARCHIBALD MACLEISH

Foreword by
FRANCIS BIDDLE

★

Essay Index Reprint Series

BOOKS FOR LIBRARIES PRESS
FREEPORT, NEW YORK

First Published 1941
Reprinted 1970

STANDARD BOOK NUMBER:
8369-1449-X

LIBRARY OF CONGRESS CATALOG CARD NUMBER:
74-104995

*

List of Contributors

DR. HANS KINDLER · LUDWIG BEMELMANS

DR. ANTON LANG · DR. CHARLES PERGLER

DR. THOMAS MANN · DR. RAUL D'EÇA

DR. ALBERT EINSTEIN · PETER YOLLES

JOSEPH PASTERNAK · ATTILIO PICCIRILLI

IGOR SIKORSKY · WILLIAM KNUDSEN

LOUIS ADAMIC · JUDGE FERDINAND PECORA

SENATOR ROBERT F. WAGNER · TONY SARG

DR. ALES HRDLICKA · DR. OTTO STRUVE

CLAUDETTE COLBERT · EMIL LUDWIG

DR. STEPHEN S. WISE · GIUSEPPE BELLANCA

DR. WALTER DAMROSCH · LUISE RAINER

DR. GAETANO SALVEMINI · ELISSA LANDI

★ FOREWORD ★

by Francis Biddle

THE MEN AND WOMEN who have created this material for the Immigration and Naturalization Service of the Department of Justice are for the most part greatly distinguished in their own fields—science, the stage, music, fiction, philosophy. All of them not long ago were foreigners; all of them now are American citizens. They tell us very simply why they wanted to be Americans. The reaffirmation of the old reasons, the familiar longings, is good for all of us to hear, perhaps even most for those of us who are born and bred from the older American stock, who breathe our freedom casually, as taken for granted in our American life, and tend to forget the eager passion with which men of other nations for the past few hundred years have dreamed the American dream. President Wilson said, during the other great war, that "by the gift of the free will of independent people" this country "is constantly being renewed from generation to generation by the same process from which it was originally created."

And it is of necessity that, spoken in this sad year, there is but one theme in all these addresses—thankfulness for living in a free country. Some of the men and women who speak to us have worked here many years; others arrived but recently; but all are stirred with the same lift of the spirit because they have their being in the freedom of a democracy. Though they speak with the tongues of many races they are moved by the same aspiration—not theirs alone, but that of the anonymous and inarticulate millions who have come from foreign shores with the common faith that fuses us into a single nation.

Now we are confronted with the immediate challenge of guarding that faith. It may be difficult to share the pulse of our convictions with those for whom they do not lie as deep and close. In those other times which stirred men's minds Tom Paine shook us into unity and action. Later Walt Whitman gloried in the strength and diversity of America, which springs from that generous faith in the dignity of individual man; and Lincoln found words to express the cherished unity of the Nation. And now that the time is once more ripe, and we see clearly the choice of our country—the whole of our past and future fusing, as it were, in this single instant—those things which we long to hear will be said again, unforgettably, for ourselves and for those who come after us.

★ INTRODUCTION ★

by Archibald MacLeish

THIS BOOK HAD ITS ORIGIN in broadcasts by some of the most distinguished of naturalized Americans. They were given on a program prepared by the Immigration and Naturalization Service of the United States Department of Justice. The purpose of the program was in part to reply to those in this and in other countries who make political capital of the differences of race and the suspicion of strangers, in part to remind Americans of all bloods and all origins that America was once, and must still remain, the land to which the lovers of freedom, the refugees from intolerance, the fighters for liberty of man and mind, can always turn.

I was asked to give the first broadcast on this program, not because I am a naturalized American, for I am not. I was born in Cook County in Illinois of a Scottish father and a mother whose people have been Americans for more than three hundred years. I was asked to give the first broadcast because I had written a poem called *America Was Promises* which concerned itself with this country and the people who came to it.

The meaning of the title of the poem was this: that America from the very beginning—from the first knowledge men had of it—was promises. It was a promise of wealth, of well-being, of escape, of freedom, of new beginnings. It was such a promise to all men who heard of it, whether by signs at sea or by discovery along its coasts, or by water and grass as they went west across it. And like all promises, it was a promise which men believed would come true of itself. Like the promises in the fairy tales.

This was the meaning of the title of the poem. And the meaning of the poem itself is that the promises do not come true of themselves—that they must be made to come true—that they must be made to come true by men.

To say this, the poem tells of those to whom the promises were made. There was Columbus first, who saw the promise made by the floating branch upon the seawater, the birds, the rain. There were the Spaniards of Cortes, landing on the coast, moving westward toward Mexico, toward Colua, toward the promise of the silver moon and the golden sun sent them from beyond these mountains. There was Thomas Jefferson who saw the spiritual promises of a new world of the human spirit, and thought they were promises made to the idea, the ideal of Man.

There was John Adams who saw the fat farms, the busy trade, of the new Republic, and thought their promises were made to the well-to-do and the intelligent—the Aristocracy of Wealth and Talents. There was Tom Paine who saw the wild American shore and the vast American forests and thought the promises of those high American horizons were promises made to all men everywhere.

The poem tells of these men and how the promise did not come true of itself for any of them.

And it tells of us and of what we have learned about the promises in our time—what we have learned in Austria and Czechoslovakia and Poland and Spain and Holland and France—that unless the people of a country, the whole people of a country, make the promises come true for the sake of the people, others will make them come true. And not for the sake of the people. For the sake of others.

In this small book are the words of those who have learned these things for themselves—who know of their own knowledge what America promises and who know too the danger in which these promises now stand. It is a book which many Americans will wish to read for understanding as well as for remembrance.

★ ACKNOWLEDGEMENT ★

"I am an American!"—These words were never more important than in these vital moments of world crisis and bloodshed. To give this magic sentence the importance it truly deserves and to introduce the noted new Americans whose lives it has affected, the United States Department of Justice has prepared the nationwide series of radio interviews on which this little volume is based. To the U. S. Department of Justice and to Dorothy Donnell, director of Americanization programs for the *Immigration and Naturalization Service,* who has been responsible for the program and in a large measure for this book, the editor offers his sincere thanks and acknowledgement.

It is with great pleasure that all of the people concerned with the writing and editing of this book have assigned their royalties to the American Red Cross.

R. S. B.

I AM AN AMERICAN

★ 1 ★

by Dr. Hans Kindler

I WAS BORN in Rotterdam, Holland and in 1914 I exchanged one good country for another. I came to America.

My trip over here at that time was only to visit my mother, who was in New York. Then the War started and kept me from returning. I took out my first papers when I joined a musicians' union to earn my living, playing the 'cello with the Philadelphia Symphony. I applied for my final papers out of gratitude and loyalty to a country which had been so generous to a strange boy. I would not accept its benefits without its responsibilities. And I know that I did well. I am glad that my children are Americans, not only for what America now is, but for what it can some day be.

In troubled times like these, with emotions and prejudices on the loose, and much of the world at war, people's liberties can be jeopardized. There is a very true sentence engraved on the portal of one of our government buildings on Constitution Avenue. Every American should say it to himself every day. It is this: "Eternal vigilance is the price of Liberty."

Things are happening very fast nowadays. Many people all over the world are losing—almost overnight—rights and ideals that have taken perhaps hundreds of years to win. We in America can't protect democracy by remembering it just on a few national holidays and taking it for granted the other three hundred and sixty days a year!

No good American contends that the United States has developed all of its possibilities yet. There are frontiers ahead of us still . . . frontiers of better standards of living for all, for example.

A democracy never stops growing—or if it does, it stops being a democracy. Your wise Jefferson and Franklin wrote the Constitution to provide for such growth and to fit the future as well as the conditions of their own day. I remember reading of Benjamin Franklin's curiosity about the future of America and how he cried once to his grandson that he wished he might be preserved in a cask of spirits so that he could see what the new country would be like after three hundred years.

That was only a hundred and fifty years ago, so another hundred and fifty years must pass before the great philosopher's curiosity can be satisfied. But, in the meantime, the Constitution which he helped to draft has been found to contain good answers to most of our important

4

national questions—with very few amendments, although our American life has changed so vastly during the same period.

In so many European countries the pattern of life is finished. There is no room in their plan of government for gradual change. So, if they are lucky, they remain at a standstill. And if they are not so lucky, they are violently overthrown.

America is still moving toward ideals, just as she was in Jefferson's day. These are the same ideals, Liberty, Equality, individual responsibility, Justice—perhaps these things are too great ever to be fully realized. And these rights must always be won, and re-won. We may not be so much nearer our great goals than we were a hundred and fifty years ago. But the important thing is that we should still be moving toward them with strong purpose and determination. That is why I would have all Americans stop and take stock, as we Americans say. Civil liberties are not possessions we can shut away in a desk drawer and say, "There they are—safe. We can forget them until we will them to our children." We must be always examining them to see that they are still in good working order. At least, that is how it seems to me.

Many people ask me if I have ever felt a spirit of antagonism among many Americans toward all aliens, including foreign-born citizens, but I have never felt it. From the first day I came here I have found good friends in this country, not only among Holland-Americans but all Americans everywhere I have been. But I think perhaps I know what people mean when they say that. America sometimes does ask of its foreign-born citizens that they forget their backgrounds and old ways as soon as possible. I think that there she impoverishes herself. This is an international world we live in nowadays, and growing smaller all the time. If a nation is to live at close quarters with other nations, she would be wise to know as much as possible about her neighbors and their culture, economics, political views and habits of thinking so as to get along with them peaceably. Here we have Americans whose parents came—or who came themselves —from every part of the globe. Through our foreign-born citizens we could know the viewpoints, languages, needs of every country. We would be the best-informed nation in the world, and we could surely plan our own course more wisely; like a farmer who listens to the weather predictions and is ready for storms when they come.

What a waste it would be to throw away the possibilities which come freely to this country in every ship, possibilities of understanding and beauty. Take the matter of language, for instance. Of course the foreign-born citizen must learn English as quickly as possible for his own sake, but why should he make such panic-stricken haste to discard his own tongue? I know many second-generation Americans who cannot speak a word of their parents' native language! I should be sorry if my own children were to be deprived of the great classics of their own and other people's ancestors. And there again America impoverishes herself. We could and should speak many languages, naturally, easily, and so understand all peoples better than we do.

Too often we think of our foreign-born citizens as living in foreign colonies in our big cities—as reading foreign-language newspapers—as representing unassimilated groups of strangers among our population. But these conditions have been changing rapidly. That, at least, is one good thing the Depression has done for America! It has given people more community life, drawn them closer together. Before 1929 everyone was in a hurry, hurry to get ahead and advance his own interests! Even the people on the street seemed always going to keep some important engagement. We had no time to stop to listen to the other fellow's troubles. Now it is different. I believe we Americans are thinking about each other's problems more sympathetically than we have at any time since I came to this country in 1914.

It was not until we were made equal by insecurity and hard times that we began to think together instead of separately, and to make laws that would help everyone. And when material things failed we turned to a more democratic form of happiness.

When I first came to this country only the wealthy could enjoy great music. Now, in the last few years, all Americans can share this joy—either free or for the cost of a movie. There is the Hollywood Bowl, and the New

York stadium, and the Philadelphia and Chicago summer symphonies and my own concerts at the Watergate last summer. Anyone who heard the great masterpieces of Wagner, Beethoven, Debussy and Gershwin played under the stars of heaven, with thousands listening on the banks of the Potomac and on the terraces of the beautiful Lincoln Memorial, or in canoes or boats, must have felt—as I did—the happiness that comes of sharing.

I was shocked when I came to Washington first to find that the Capital of one of the greatest nations in the world was without music for the people—without an orchestra even. Ever since I came to America I have wanted to do something for my new country—and now, in the National Symphony Orchestra, I have found my opportunity.

HANS KINDLER started his music studies in his native city, Rotterdam, Holland. As a boy he played with symphony orchestras in Berlin, Amsterdam, London and elsewhere. In 1914 he came to America, and when the World War broke out decided to stay here. He gave up his brilliant career as a solo cellist in 1932 and set about organizing a symphony orchestra in Washington. His National Symphony Orchestra has since become an integral part of the cultural life of the Nation's Capital and is recognized as one of the foremost of America's major symphony orchestras.

by Luise Rainer

I have been so proud in telling everyone for the last two years, "I am an American!" I have heard some people say the same words in dull, lifeless tones as if it were a matter of course to live in a country where all men are created equal and have the right to life, liberty and the pursuit of happiness! These things are not a matter of course to new Americans who have recently come from unhappier lands. To me it is a thrilling thing to be able to say that sentence with all my heart, "*I am an American!*"

I'm afraid that some native Americans take their democratic citizenship too much for granted. They pay their taxes, obey the laws and vote conscientiously but save their patriotic thoughts for national holidays like Washington's Birthday and the Fourth of July!

That is where we new Americans are more fortunate!

We have just studied the great traditions of America. We have read and reread American history and the Constitution, and we have learned in textbooks like the one the Naturalization Service gives us about the duties and privileges of being a citizen of the United States. And then we have the wonderful experience of taking the oath of allegiance and promising faithfully to defend all these great traditions and rights! That was one of the big days of my life and I think everyone else who was naturalized with me felt it also.

I was born in Germany, but my father was an American. He had taken out his papers here as a young man. Later it became necessary for business reasons for him to return to his native country and stay there. But when I was a child my favorite plea for a story was, "Tell me about America". And I said to myself always, "Some day I shall go there. Some day I shall belong".

People emigrate for many reasons, but I think because first of all they believe in the promises of democracy. They don't believe in them as traditions or ideals but as actual facts. Just like the early Spanish colonists believed they would find gold in the streets and all the streams paved with precious stones, so the new arrivals today believe that they will find equal opportunities for everyone, tolerance, justice and all the other civil liberties and rights which democracy promises actually at work in everyday life in America.

But America is still a very young country. She started

out like any young person with ideals and hopes and plans but without experience. She has to learn to live those ideas before they are really a part of her everyday life. But I think there is no danger—unless she forgets her traditions. That is why I wish that every born American might share the inspiration which we new Americans get from taking our oath of allegiance. The naturalization ceremony makes America a part of you! I think we who win it today must feel it the same way as those who won it first after the Revolution, 150 years ago. There we stood, from many lands, before the judge. We were asking so much—understanding, generosity, freedom to live and work in this country, opportunity to succeed if we deserved success. But we were promising much, too— to live according to the ideals of democracy, and to do our share to make those ideals real facts in this country. It is a very solemn thing—this oath of allegiance. All Americans should know it.

You probably have never even heard this oath of allegiance. Let me repeat it for you:

> *"I hereby declare, on oath, that I absolutely and entirely renounce and abjure all allegiance and fidelity to any foreign prince, potentate, state, or sovereignty of whom or which I was before a citizen or subject; that I will support and defend the Constitution and laws of the United States of America against all enemies, foreign or domestic; that I will bear true faith*

11

and allegiance to the same; and that I take
this obligation freely without any mental res-
ervation or purpose of evasion: So help me
God."

If all Americans realized these privileges and duties as keenly as new citizens, I think they would work harder being Americans. We should talk of Democracy and discuss its meaning and duties and problems with everyone we meet, try to understand everyone's views, and then they could never build walls around any part of the people or spread the fear and intolerance that have caused so much suffering in other countries. Such things must not be here! They would be fantastic in America—in a democracy! They go against what it says in the Constitution!

I wished to become an American because to me it is necessary to be free in order to be happy, and there is more freedom in America than anywhere else. Many of the others who were naturalized with me had different reasons, I think. I sat in the back of the room where I could watch those who were naturalized with me. The whole story of their lives and their reasons for coming to America showed in the way they raised their hands to take the oath. Some put them up slowly, as if their choice had been hard to make. Some—the younger ones—were quick, eager, as if they could hardly wait to become Americans. Some closed their hands greedily as if they

clutched at something—opportunity, perhaps, or security!
It was strange and at the same time wonderful!

I have read that other countries with different ideologies claim that Democracy doesn't inspire Youth. That it
is too "dull!" That is great nonsense. But of course Democracy *is* an adult form of government. It appeals to
people through their brains, instead of their emotions,
and most human beings have a great deal of child in
them. They love ceremony! If we are to compete with
other forms of government which cater to this universal
love of drama, it might help if we gave all our citizens—
new and old—more sense of the thrill of being Americans.

There was nothing dull about democratic ideas in
those hot days in 1787 when men and women stood
through the summer in the street outside Independence
Hall in Philadelphia waiting to hear that a Constitution
had been born! It was the chief topic of conversation
then! People talked about their beliefs, they discussed
them, and disagreed over them. What did it matter? It
kept Democracy alive! It was a part of their daily lives!
Just as it is very real and close to the new citizen today!
I am filled with pride at being an American! Often I fly
back and forth across this country, and looking out of
the windows I feel sad when it grows dark and I cannot
see more! It is such a big country. It has so much room
for people to breathe and grow! In Europe every inch of
soil that can grow food is used, even to the tops of the
mountains, but America seems hardly to have been

13

touched yet! If all the other countries use up their resources, I believe America could still support the world! And the size of the country seems a proof of safety! There is hope that it would take bad ideas too long to travel, they might die on the way.

If I go soon to Europe as I may, I shall meet and talk to many people, if I could carry any message from America not from myself, but through myself—it would make me very happy! And I shall be travelling with an American passport! I have travelled much in the different countries of Europe, and the last time there was such a difference. Everywhere I went I was received like a diplomat—or a queen—or no! Like an American citizen. Like a traveller who comes from the sweet land of liberty! That is so beautiful, isn't it—*sweet land!*

LUISE RAINER was born in Vienna and received her education in France, Switzerland and Italy, as well as in Austria. At the age of 16 she started her stage career and she was soon discovered in Vienna by a talent scout for Metro-Goldwyn-Mayer Pictures and brought to Hollywood. Among the outstanding pictures she has starred in are "The Great Ziegfeld" and "The Good Earth." She won the Motion Picture Academy Award twice in succession, in 1936 and in 1937.

by Dr. Anton Lang

PEOPLE READ AND HEAR so much about Democracy these days—I wonder whether their first reaction on seeing this word isn't to say: "More of the same old stuff!" And yet, if you stopped the average American on the street and asked him for a definition of Democracy, how many could give one offhand? I mean a really comprehensive definition that covers more than a few civil liberties and the forms of representative government?

I agree that it's vital in these troubled days for all Americans to realize the part Democracy plays in their everyday lives, but I'm only questioning whether it can be done by forcibly button-holing a man and saying, "Listen here!" and then burying him under phrases and arguments and appeals.

All your Presidents—or should I say all *our* Presidents —since the foundation of the Republic have repeated their faith in the right thinking of the people. That's what our theory of government is based on. If at this moment people need a deeper consciousness of their heritage of freedom and their own responsibilities, why not let them get it through the old tried and true American processes of education and discussion among themselves? To my mind, they must grow into it rather than be pushed in—lest they rebel!

I sometimes think that there is too much talk everywhere nowadays. A lot of the trouble in the world is being stirred up and spread by words. Millions of words around café tables, on street corners, from soap boxes. This is a time of great universal human bewilderment. So perhaps it might help us all to stop talking for a moment and collect our thoughts. Talking without thinking hurries men into impulsive actions, persecutions, prejudices, wars.

What then shall we give our people instead of words and arguments to remind them of their traditions and renew their firm determination to live by the faith of their forefathers?

Here is my suggestion—why not put Democracy into terms of human life? That is where it touches people closest, not as ideals but as everyday experience. Then through drama, motion pictures, radio programs, poetry, stories, novels, the achievements, aims and ideals of Democracy would speak to Americans today as they did to Americans when Democracy was established—through the heart and mind, and not through the poor long-suffering ears! Too many people, I find, think of Democracy more in theoretical terms, instead of translating them into practice.

The enemies of Democracy claim that it is too slow a process for times of crisis and quick change but I think that we still have time for thinking in this country. In comparison, America is too happy to fear justly, sudden change.

In most respects America is the happiest country in the world today. Let's hope that it will stay that way. Happiness, security, human dignity—such human values have suddenly become the criteria for the world instead of the more material standards. The hope of these things is what has been drawing people here from other lands. Once perhaps they came with the dream of getting rich, now they think of America as the one country where people can still hope. I have never yet met an American who would admit that he was down and out, they always pick themselves up and go on again.

People in Europe find their position in life more or less fixed while in America, by our customs, and traditions, and the very democratic conception, people have something to look ahead to—by which I mean, life seems to be so much more flexible in the new world than abroad. The size and make-up of this country still offers opportunities undreamed of in Europe where every inch of earth has been cultivated for centuries and farmers cut the grass around railroad tie and post and tree so that not a blade is wasted. We are a long way from that here. People can hope to better their standards of living and advance in their jobs. There is still the tang of adventure left in life over here, yes, and plenty of it!

The more obvious frontiers are closed now, of course. But there are frontiers of thought, and of fuller life for everyone which men may still strive for here with the hope of achieving them. Where liberties within limits remain, progress remains, for even freedom is relative— never absolute. We speak confidently of our liberties without examining them—whether we really possess them as fully as we think or not. Democracy is an experience— like religion—it has to be renewed by every generation —by every citizen. It is growing, not fixed. You can't look at it as something that was won once and for all, a hundred and fifty years ago, and that will always be there when it is needed. To every American it should be as personal as it is to all new Americans.

I think in some cases new Americans are more conscious of our liberties and traditions—and perhaps our responsibilities—than many citizens of longer standing, because for many centuries they have brought this longing for intellectual and religious liberty and economic opportunity with them from less favored lands. That is the safety of America! The human needs and hopes on which the nation was founded are renewed with every immigrant that has arrived since then! If only older

Americans would try to understand the attitude found in the people who have chosen America for their home! The foreign-born who come to America to be naturalized ask only to be allowed to adjust themselves to the life here as quickly as possible. They are eager to learn the ways of their new home. They are looking ahead, not back. But the Americans they meet often do not help them make this adjustment. Instead they keep them foreign by an attitude of curiosity. If harmful alien ideas of government and of living do come into America from abroad it is partly because people here question newcomers so eagerly about conditions in other countries and their old life which often they are anxious to forget—naturally, everyone is expected to feel attached to his native soil and cherishes dear memories of the beauties of his homeland and the loved ones he leaves behind, as I do, together with thousands of other newcomers.

The government through its co-operation with naturalization schools and other agencies is trying to help the new citizen take his place in the pattern of normal American life as quickly as possible. But do these schools—do any of our schools—teach persistently the real meaning of good citizenship? In most colleges Government is an elective course. I think that very few native Americans realize from infancy what their part in a democratic life should be, or are taught to question whether life in the United States is moving toward our traditional Democracy or away from it. Most of us seem to follow the gen-

19

eral trend without much thought. I wish that such things might be impressed more on new Americans than they were when I was naturalized in 1932.

Though I liked America from the first, it was nevertheless a solemn step to change my nationality, and it took me five years to make up my mind to become a citizen. When I was sure that I wished to spend the remainder of my life in this country, and bring up my family and build my home here, I applied for my first papers. At last all formalities and steps were finished and finally the great day came. With awe and anticipation in our hearts, my wife and I went to the address where I was to take the oath of allegiance.

Those who were to be naturalized—about fifty-three of us—were crowded into the courtroom where the event was to take place. The clerk raced through the administration of the oath while the Judge looked on, then told us to file into the hall and pay for our certificates. And that was all! As we went out into the street, there was an ache in my heart. I had looked ahead so long to this day, and it was so different from my dreams!

True, the picture has changed a little since then for the Immigration and Naturalization Service is now trying to provide for a more dignified setting and ceremony for welcoming our new citizens. In some cities, such as Cleveland, naturalization is already impressive and beautiful.

But I do think there is too much talk today, too many

speeches, too much argument, and theorizing, and too many warnings and threats—but I don't think there is enough education along certain lines. If Democracy is to endure, it must depend on the considered thought of the people, and the exchange of ideas. And ideas to be useful must have a background of information. The new citizen is required to know American history, the Constitution, something about our form of government, but this is the letter of Democracy, not the spirit. To become a good American we must understand our own personal relation to Democracy. If the new American just entering on citizenship is not given this deeper consciousness of all that Americanism implies, the native-born citizen has even less chance of having these things brought home to him, it seems to me.

I feel when I look at America as one feels looking at all young things. I am afraid that unless we take every possible precaution, suffering may be ahead for it—though not from without, but from within. A friend of mine in a European country where his church is fighting for its existence at the moment wrote me a letter recently, "We never knew how much our faith meant to us until we had to suffer for it." And just so we have to cherish and protect our democratic ideals. It may be that America is destined to preserve civilization for humanity. To reveal Democracy not against a background of blood and smoke, but to let its heartwarming rays shine out into the world from a beacon that stands for good will, and happiness for all . . . this would be a great destiny!

ANTON LANG was born in 1905 at Oberammergau, Germany where several generations of his family had become noted for their presentation of the famous Passion Play. In 1926 he accepted a scholarship at Holy Cross College, Worcester, Mass. After his return to Europe, Georgetown University offered him a professorship. He accepted this in 1932 and has been living in this country ever since. All of his four children have been born in the United States.

by Dr. Charles Pergler

WHENEVER I'VE BEEN DESCRIBED as a naturalized citizen it always surprises me. I have lived in this country so much of my life that I am sure no one could feel more American than I do. Still there is a difference between myself and many native Americans. I find that I am more interested in the foreign-born citizen than they are. That's one reason why I'm glad to write this—because, having been born in Czechoslovakia and brought up in America, I see both sides of the situation and perhaps may be able to suggest some new aspects on the problem of the stranger within our gates.

Immigration is a problem to the Nation and its new citizens. The stranger within our gates has always been a problem in any country in every age. And when the stranger has come to stay in this country it is to his interest as well as to those who admitted him that he stop being a stranger as soon as possible. I think that the immigrant has been a problem in the United States much longer than was necessary because the process of fitting him into the life of the country was unduly delayed.

Easing the newcomer into the rich stream of American life calls for tolerance and patience on the part of the American people. And tolerance is the first of the democratic virtues! But in the past, foreign-born citizens have sometimes been regarded with condescension and even suspicion by the older element, or ignored completely. Naturally, that drove them to seek the society of others of their own origin. And so we have Italian quarters, and German districts in our big American cities and naturalized citizens of many years' standing who can hardly speak to their neighbors because they have never learned their adopted language. These racial groups had no real connection with American life . . . except for the part they played in ward politics and the clambakes given for them round election time!

I think we could trace much of the corruption in some big cities directly to the helplessness of the foreign-born resident and his necessary reliance on the only people who held out their hands to him in this strange new life—often a cheap type of machine politician. "Boss-ism" is always an undemocratic thing and many a boss in the old days owed his power to the fact that foreign-born Americans were abandoned to his care by fellow citizens whose first duty should have been to introduce them to the healthy features of American life. Also, at times the situation resulted in exploitation of the immigrant by the more unscrupulous of his own kind.

I got my education in the schools of a large American city, but the Americanization of Charles Pergler didn't take place in Chicago, but in a small country town where I lived for a number of years. You know the type of place, one sleepy street with a town square in front of the courthouse, where the old men sit in the sun and exchange ideas and everyone stops to greet each other and talk over the town news. I sometimes go back there and join them, even today. It is in towns like this that traditional Democracy still flourishes as it did in the colonial days of the town meetings. People are interested in each other and understand each other.

But in our great cities there are no village greens which form natural meeting places for the people. Families live side by side for years in some big modern apartment house without ever learning each other's name. And of course there are even fewer opportunities for new Americans to get acquainted with the older element. The organization of modern urban American society doesn't cherish and protect Democracy by offering much chance for the exchange of ideas, and mutual understanding. Most foreign-born Americans are used to talking—that's the chief amusement back in the old country, around café tables, in their singing societies, in their homes. But in the great American cities people don't casually drift together to discuss their affairs. When they meet it is to promote some group interest or cause, or as spectators at baseball games or the movies. And so the newcomer, anxious to understand his new country and to share its life, learns to be a spectator too and drifts willy-nilly toward his own racial groups for companionship. It is not his fault. Perhaps it is nobody's fault. But it is very unfortunate.

The immigrant has never presented a serious problem in the rural districts. Many of our States were settled and developed by groups from other countries who have merged entirely today with the rest of their communities. And they have made real contributions to American life too, not only materially, but spiritually, wherever their neighbors have come to know them well. After all, naturalization is not merely a matter of legal form—the newcomer must become part and parcel of American life—and the sooner he learns to speak English, and think and feel in democratic terms, the better for all concerned!

I was struck with the remark of a speaker at the recent meeting of the League for the Protection of the Foreign Born; he said, "Who are the foreigners in this country? I don't know anything more American myself than a Greek restaurant, or an Italian fruit stand, or a Chinese laundry—do you?" We're all foreigners, if we go back far enough.

History should teach us that, if our democratic tradition of tolerance doesn't! I think we do have more tolerance here right now than elsewhere in the world. But it seems to me that real Democracy is possible only in homogeneous nations—which possess what we might call like-mindedness. It isn't enough for Americans of different nationalities to live on the same street. It isn't enough for newcomers to obtain their citizenship papers. The safety of Democracy demands Americanization in spirit. And that can't be accomplished by standing aloof from our new citizens or worse—abandoning them to elements quite unrepresentative of what is best in America. Let those who complain of un-American activities ask themselves whether they are ever guilty of that most un-American vice—intolerance!

Segregation and differentiation should be avoided above all. You've heard the saying: God gives us our relatives, thank God we can choose our friends! But our country gives us some of our fellow citizens and as Americans it is necessary for us to do everything humanly possible to make them a normal and useful part of the community life.

As a lawyer I should say that the alien is better off in this country than anywhere else in the world. I will go even further and say that the United States is probably the only country which constitutionally guarantees to every person, foreign-born or native-born, the equal protection of its laws. Since there is no legal distinction between a naturalized and a native American, there should be no distinctions of any other kind—even the term "foreign-born" differentiates them! Whether we like it or not, the immigrant once naturalized is a part of American life and leaves his mark on it.

Of course there shouldn't be any such things as Italian-Americans, or Irish-Americans or Polish-Americans or any hyphenated Americans at all, but taking a realistic view you must admit that the newly naturalized citizen is faced with problems and needs that do put him into a minority group, at least for a while. And the defense of the rights of minorities is certainly a traditional American duty and one which is especially necessary to the safety of a democracy. But I'm not so certain that it is desirable to form special organizations for the defense of the foreign-born. It only calls attention to the fact that they are different and segregates them into a group. After all, the naturalized citizens' problems are American problems, his rights are American rights, and his defense and assimilation is an American interest. If his rights are in danger, doesn't it suggest that the constitutional guarantees of all of us may be equally in danger?

All Americans should be vigilant to protect their own rights—and not merely the rights of minorities because there is no telling when our opinions or interests may put us into a minority grouping. If we have ever needed understanding and tolerance in our own lives we should not tolerate intolerance toward others. It's a changed attitude toward the foreign-born that the problem calls for, not more laws or organizations.

DR. CHARLES PERGLER

CHARLES PERGLER was born in Czechoslovakia and first came to the United States in May, 1890. After his graduation from Chicago public schools he returned to Prague with his mother, returning again to Chicago in 1903. There he was active as a Czech journalist and law student, receiving a Bachelor of Laws degree in 1908 and being admitted to the Bar in the same year. Soon after this he started his own law practice in Iowa. Now a member of the District of Columbia Bar, Dr. Pergler is Dean of the National University Law School and an authority on International Law.

★ 5 ★

by D. Thomas Mann

FAMILIAR SURROUNDINGS mean much to a writer . . . his own desk, his accustomed books and walls, the view from the window of his study, which meets his eyes when he lifts them from his work. . . . People often tell me that I must have great faith and hope in Democracy as a way of living to resign all these things and deliberately choose America as my future homeland. That is certainly true. No, I have not been disappointed in America. Here I am sure that I have found a second home where I can continue my life's work in peace and freedom for people in America have been hospitable to me and to my ideas as well.

In spite of recent events abroad, and the statement that one sometimes hears today, "Perhaps Democracy is too slow a process for a crisis," my faith in this idea as a way of life in a modern mechanized world has not faltered. Far from it. I still have a profound faith in freedom. I once expressed this faith in a little book called *The Coming Victory Of Democracy* in which I connected Democracy with the highest human attributes; with the dignity of mankind, with truth and with justice. Democracy wishes to raise up mankind, to give it freedom, and its greatest strength lies in its deep spiritual and moral self-consciousness.

We hear so much defeatist talk today in some countries about outworn forms of government, and young vigorous modern ideologies with which the enemies of Democracy have sought to trick us. In an effort to force their will upon the masses they despise, these foes present their ideas as something new and revolutionary. They assert that justice and freedom are outgrown in this modern world. Sincere and honest people allow themselves to wonder whether this may not be true. Force, hate, cruelty, fear—are these things new or modern? The idea of Democracy is eternal, but its forms are changeable and must be changed.

I am sure, however, that Democracy *can* adapt itself to the requirements of world trade, technological unemployment, economic troubles which beset humanity in this industrial age. As we all know, great economic changes have already been made in democratic countries in the last 10 years. The United States in particular has made remarkable progress toward the solution of some of the great problems which face us today.

Americans are sometimes accused of offering no constructive program which will enlist the eager loyalties of youth. But I wouldn't quite agree with that. I would think that a realization of the social progress America has made in the last 10 years might well stir the imagination of youth. Perhaps, there is need for this progress to be presented to the young people in a more forcible and attractive way. There is no reason why Democracy should not enlighten its people by all the modern means at its disposal, by propaganda even, for today more than ever, Democracy's task is to defend civilization against barbarism. There is no doubt that young people are deeply impressed by the outward successes of the so-called totalitarian governments, and therefore it is imperative that we do all in our power to uphold and strengthen the faith of youth in our American form of government. I would like everybody, young and old, to realize that there can be no human dignity, individual happiness, justice or security, when the true ideals of Democracy are lacking. We who have come to America from Europe have seen how easily the highest motives and ideals of youth can be exploited by unscrupulous despots and made to serve the lowest kind of political strategy.

No one could live in America as long as my family and I have, without realizing that America is the possessor of a definite national unity, a communal spirit of loyalty peculiar to itself. This national characteristic is to be found as surely in the men and women who are recent arrivals in America as in the Americans whose forebears have lived here for generations.

Every nation is apt to fear that its national character will be weakened if it permits extensive immigration. But I have the utmost faith that in America the absorption and assimilation of immigrants is nearly inexhaustible. The Swedes, the Danes, the Germans who came to this country from Europe in former years, pioneered for America and helped build its cities and develop its lands. History shows that Americans need not fear that foreign-born citizens will remain foreign. They have always sought to become true Americans as quickly as possible.

America is more thickly settled today but to us who have come from overcrowded lands abroad, America still seems to have a great deal of room. I read recently that if a cultivated acre in America had to support as many people as a cultivated acre in my former country, then the United States would have a population of 485,000,000 people. One has only to think of Alaska, to realize that America still has rich and great lands to open up. And is it not possible that it might be a real advantage to the United States if these rich economic possibilities were developed?

Some say that if we dictate where refugees shall settle when they come to America we shall be interfering with their freedom of action. I do not think that this is necessarily so for I believe that today the concept of freedom is changing. Nowadays we should be adjusting individual

33

claims by friendly and willing concessions to the claims of all. Let me put it very simply. If I am free to play my radio all night, then others lose their freedom to sleep. Do you see what I mean? Americans have already adjusted themselves to a great degree to this voluntary limitation of personal freedom for the common good.

Americans are very reasonable and charitable, I would say. Owing to the strong Puritan origins of this country, the Christian feeling for life underlies the practical, matter-of-fact spirit which is inherent in the American character. This mixture of Christian feeling and practical power makes the people of this great country especially well fitted to make the adjustments necessary to secure spiritual as well as economic freedom. For instance, I do not think freedom of speech should be permitted to those who would use it to our harm. Democracy's concept of freedom must never include the freedom to destroy it.

I earnestly think that there has never been such a threat to freedom in the world as at present. A victory for the present forces of evil in Europe would mean the end of all personal freedom everywhere. I cannot discuss America's role in preserving civilization without mentioning this fundamental fact. But if I think that the defeat of Hitler is the basic condition for freedom and justice on earth, it does not mean that I feel America should cease to strive endlessly for the social and economic betterment of its people here at home. In other countries intolerable conditions, unemployment, and unsolved problems and unmet needs have provided a fertile soil for the seeds of danger and retrogression.

Democracy can and will triumph. There would be no hope for Europe, if as a result of this war, there should not be established a Democracy of free peoples who are responsible each one to the other—a European Federation in fact. This may sound impossible of achievement today, yet it is not too early to hold out such a solution to mankind. Already in many countries men are thinking along these lines. America may yet stand forth in an abandoned and ethically leaderless world as the preserver of a faith which is proved sound and utterly necessary to human life, faith in goodness, in freedom and truth, in justice and peace. Only so is there any hope for the world.

THOMAS MANN'S birthplace was Lubeck, Germany in 1875. In the intervening years he became one of Europe's best-known writers. Dr. Mann was for many years a member of the Prussian Academy and in 1929 was awarded the Nobel Prize for Literature. Among his many noted books are "The Magic Mountain" and "Joseph In Egypt." Several years ago he and his family left Germany to make their permanent home in the United States. He now lives in California with his family where he is continuing his brilliant literary career as an American citizen.

★ 6 ★

by Attilio Piccirilli

I HAVE BEEN an American for so long—50 years—that I often forget that I was born in Italy. When anyone refers to me as a foreigner, or as an Italian, I pretend that I haven't heard and I don't usually answer. Of course I am an American—Look!

Once, when I thought that I would like to travel a little, I went back to my native city and planned to stay there for a year or more. I locked the door of my studio in New York City, said goodbye to all of my friends and went back to the homeland where I had been born. What did I find?

I was a foreigner in Italy. I could speak the language, of course, but I couldn't think Italian. All of my thoughts were those of an American. I had planned to be away a year but in four weeks I was on my return trip to the Bronx.

My brother and I first came over here together. I shan't tell you how old we were for that is not important. We were boys, with big eyes—boys leaning over the boat rail watching New York harbor. I had twenty-five cents in my pocket, I remember, and my brother and I discussed whether, if our uncle didn't meet us that day, it would be enough to buy some bread and cheese.

There's one big difference right there. Today we wouldn't be allowed to land in America with 25 cents in our pockets! They were glad to have us come in those days for there weren't enough Americans to do the work over here. And there's another difference.

I had raised a beard in honor of America for I wanted to look impressive. But I was so young that the result was not as impressive as I had hoped—with a bunch of hair here, and some there. My uncle *was* there to meet us with a friend. Right away they led us off to show us all of the sights. First we went to Castle Gardens. It's the Aquarium now.

Everyone had a clean shirt and a shaved face, and I asked my uncle, "What day is today?" "Tuesday" he told me.

"No. No," I said. "I mean what fete day is it! Everybody is washed and wearing white shirts—it must be a great national holiday!"

My uncle and his friend laughed. "Oh," they told us, "it isn't a fete day. People wear clean shirts every day in America." I was more impressed by that than anything they showed me. Two days later I took out my first citizenship papers, and I think that I have been a good American ever since.

I first *knew* that I was a real American when I brought my mother's body back from Italy where she had died on a visit. We buried her here and I made a statue of motherhood for her grave. I had worked here, and succeeded a little, and taken the oath of allegiance. But it is when you bury one you love in a country's soil that you realize that you belong to that soil forever.

From the beginning I was happy here. I had my work and the friend of my uncle who met us at the boat was good to us. He gave us money to send for my mother and the others, and when they came he rented an apartment and bought furniture. He didn't know whether or not we would ever pay him back, but he took a chance, as we Americans say. He was Jewish and a fine American.

Schools are always asking me to speak to them, and what do they want me to talk to them about? "How I succeeded!" As if you could make a rule for success. And anyhow who says that I have succeeded?

Have I made a big fortune? No. But I have had a good life. I've worked hard from the first, and earned plenty of money, and spent it and been happy. For five years my brother Furio and I only put our mallets and chisels down to eat and sleep. We did not know whether we were making money with our sculpture or not. We didn't even think of money. My parents were good business

people and they managed everything, the sale of our
work, buying our house in the Bronx, everything! I
noticed that we had more furniture as time went on, and
we ate better food, but I never knew that in those first
five years my brother and I had earned over $50,000.
Perhaps that is the only possible rule for success as an
artist—not to think of work in terms of money, but of
opportunity and of joy.

I am often asked if I think that a young artist coming
to this country now would still find it a land of opportunity? Yes, I do. There is as much opportunity here
now as there was when I came, if the people could only
see it. Cities and towns and villages from coast to coast
and every one of them needing to be beautified. At first
everybody was too busy making a country out of wilderness to think of beauty! They built ugly houses and
buildings which could be put up in a hurry. Now it must
all be done over again. I'm tired of hearing people talk
as if America was finished. What has been done? Not
much that doesn't need to be torn down and done over
again as you know if you've ever traveled in America
and have seen its small towns.

There's work for everybody in rebuilding America.
Work for carpenters and bricklayers and factory hands,
and house painters—and work for the artist, too! We are
just awakening to the idea of adorning our homes and
schoolhouses and public buildings with frescoes and
paintings and sculpture. And yet with a whole nation

to make over, with 130,000,000 people to supply with the good modern things of living we talk as if there never would be enough jobs any more. The young artist who comes to America today, or who is born in America has plenty of opportunity. But opportunity is not all outside, you know. It is inside the heart too so we must carry our own opportunity with us. That is why I have had my art school here in New York for thirty years—so that all young people who carry opportunity in their hearts shall find the door open to them. There is no trouble becoming a pupil of Attilio Piccirilli. All a girl or boy has to do is open my door and step inside. I'll tell them, "There is the clay. There is a hook. Hang up your hat and go to work." Then they are my pupils.

Art does not need to be encouraged—just given a chance. That's why the tuition in my school is $1 a year, and why I ask to see no samples of applicants' work. It is enough that one has the desire to paint or model in his soul and anyone with this desire is better off in America today than in any other country. People say that America has no traditions for the artist. So much the better. When I was a boy in Italy and went to art classes, —they always talked about Michelangelo. They held that great master up so much as a model that it discouraged a beginner! He must be like Michelangelo. That was a bit too much to expect. There is more freedom for creative effort in this country without old masters to live up to, and as for great talent—no, I haven't found much. There really isn't much in the world.

Why then do I continue to run my school? It does take some time away from my work. I'll tell you why—America has given me everything and this is a way I can pay her back a little, every day. As a sculptor I haven't gotten very rich but as an American I *am* very rich—and that is the way I want to be thought of. A few years ago they made me very proud by giving me a medal of honor for my contribution to America as an artist. Governor Pollard of Virginia made a speech when he gave it to me and called me a great sculptor.

"Governor Pollard," I said, "Will you please change what you have just said. I would rather you called me a 'good American' than a great sculptor."

America's gifts are all good so I cannot say what is the greatest gift America has given me. Opportunity I have already spoken of. Freedom of speech—that's an important one. When I go to other countries I sometimes forget and say what I please. Then only my American passport has saved me from some bad moments. I could never live in a country where I must weigh every word before I say it for fear of trouble. Justice, that's important too. But I think that the feeling of equality, of being just as good as anyone else is the greatest gift America has to offer naturalized citizens. It is like the day I arrived here and saw all the people wearing clean shirts, not just the rich. It makes a newcomer feel that he can do anything and be anybody. It makes him hold his head high, and work with a will to succeed in this new land.

After fifty years I still feel this same sense of equality. I have known almost everyone in my lifetime, it seems. Caruso used to come to my house and sit at my kitchen table and sing to me alone. Teddy Roosevelt sat at the same table and ate the spaghetti I cooked. Everyone has been my friend, policemen and politicians and presidents and bricklayers and the children who play ball on the street and break my windows. They are all my friends! Where else in the world can that be true? Nowhere except in America.

ATTILIO PICCIRILLI was born in 1866 in Massa-Carrara, a picturesque town in the hills of Tuscany. Like his father before him, young Piccirilli and his five brothers grew up to be sculptors. He began a six-year course at the Royal Academy of Fine Arts in Rome at the age of thirteen and in 1887 he went to London with one of his brothers. The following year found them in America. Within a few years Attilio Piccirilli had an international reputation as a master sculptor. His work has ranged from the Maine Memorial and the John McDonogh Memorial monuments to the world's first monumental glass sculpture in Rockefeller Center. He is President of the Leonardo da Vinci Art School which he has helped finance for many years for the benefit of the under-privileged who wish to study art.

42

by Dr. Albert Einstein

MY SUBJECT, of course, is Democracy but I must say that I do not think words alone will solve humanity's present problems. The sound of bombs drowns out men's voices. In ordinary times—times of peace—I have great faith in the communication of ideas between thinking men, but today I am afraid the intellectual way to appeal to men is fast becoming of little avail with brute force dominating so many million lives.

Seven years ago, when asked for the reason why I had given up my position in Germany—I made this statement: "As long as I have any choice I will only stay in a country where political liberty, toleration, and equality of all citizens before the law is the rule. Political liberty implies liberty to express one's political opinion orally and in writing, and a tolerant respect for any and every individual opinion."

Making allowances for human imperfections, I do feel that in America the most valuable thing in life is possible, the development of the individual and his creative powers. There may be men who can live without political rights and without opportunity of free individual development. But I think that this is intolerable for most Americans. Here, for generations, men have never been under the humiliating necessity of unquestioning obedience. Here human dignity has been developed to such a point that it would be impossible for people to endure life under a system in which the individual is only a slave of the State and has no voice in his government and no decision on his own way of life. We simply will not be driven about like sheep, we are independent. We are self-reliant. We do not know what it means to be deferential to class or position. Fortunately for us "obey" is a little heard word, and "co-operate" is a common one.

I think from what I have seen of Americans since I have come here, they are not suited by temperament or tradition for existence under a totalitarian system. I think that most of them would not find life worth living in that way. Therefore, it is very important that they consider how these liberties that are so necessary to them may be preserved and defended. Americans can and must co-operate because nothing truly valuable can be achieved except by the unselfish cooperation of many individuals.

In my own field science has provided the possibility of liberation for human beings from hard labor, but science itself is not a liberator. It creates means, not goals. Men should use them for reasonable goals. When the ideals of humanity are war and conquest, those tools become as dangerous as a razor in the hands of a child of three. We must not condemn man's inventiveness and patient conquest of the forces of nature because they are being used wrongly and destructively now. The fate of humanity is entirely dependent upon its moral development.

I think it is quite understandable that leaders in science and culture had so little influence on the course of political events. Scientists and artists through their works frequently have had enduring influence even in the realm of politics. But in order to influence the course of political events directly one must also have the gift to influence people and their actions directly. This is rather a matter of arousing and using emotions and personal confidence than of clear understanding of causal connections. For this reason intellectuals have little chance to impress an audience. Also they usually do not have the gift to make decisions swiftly.

Among the outstanding American statesmen Woodrow Wilson is perhaps the truest example of the intellectual type. But he too did not seem to have mastered the art of dealing with men. His greatest achievement, the League of Nations, appears today as a failure on superficial observation. But in spite of the mutilation by his contemporaries and the boycott by his fellow-countrymen, Wilson's work in my opinion will be re-created in a more powerful form. *Then* only will the importance of this Great Innovator be fully recognized.

Yet I am convinced that a Federal organization of the nations of the world is not only possible but even an absolute necessity if the conditions on our planet are not to become unbearable for men. The League of Nations failed because its members were not willing to give up a part of their rights of sovereignty and because the League was without any executive power. A world organization cannot insure peace effectively unless it has control over the whole military power of its members.

Exaggerated nationalism is an artificially created emotional state resulting from the necessity to be prepared for war. This exaggerated nationalism would quickly disappear with the elimination of the war-danger. I do not believe that the unequal geographical distribution of raw materials must necessarily lead to wars. As long as a nation has access to the materials which are necessary for its development, it can very well prosper. This is clearly shown by nations such as Switzerland, Finland, Denmark and Norway, which belonged to the most prosperous countries of Europe before the war. One of the most important functions of such an international organization would be to secure unhampered distribution of the raw materials and free access to the markets. The solution of the internal economical and social problems could be left largely to the individual states. I am far from optimistic for what I have said is not a prophecy but a statement of what must be done to prevent life on this earth from becoming unbearable.

Everybody will agree that we are now further removed from this goal than seemed to be the case ten years ago. This setback could have been avoided if the Democracies had then shown the same solidarity and readiness for sacrifice they are showing now in this hour of grave emergency. Will to sacrifice, solidarity and wise foresight, however, are most effective *before* the hour of dire necessity has arrived. May our America be spared such an hour through the resolute action of her citizens and statesmen.

ALBERT EINSTEIN, one of the world's foremost scientists, was born at Ulm, in Southern Germany, in 1879. He spent his childhood in Bavaria and received his education in Switzerland where he later became a citizen. From 1902 until 1909 he was an engineer in the Swiss Federal Patent Office. He then became a professor of theoretical physics at various noted European Universities and from 1914 until the early part of 1933 was a member of the Prussian Academy of Sciences in Berlin. Since 1933, and the Nazi Inquisition, Dr. Einstein has been a member of the faculty of the Institute of Advanced Study, at Princeton, N. J. He became a U. S. citizen in October 1940.

★ **8** ★

by Peter Yolles

THE NEWSPAPER I edit is the *Nowy Swiat,* but it is significant to note that we never speak of it as Polish. We always say that it is an American newspaper printed in the Polish language. I think you would find few other papers in the United States more conscious of American traditions and responsibilities than ours. That is naturally so, since the purpose of the *Nowy Swiat* is to explain America to newcomers to this country and so help them to take their place in life here. I have often been asked whether I think that foreign language publications delay the assimilation of these newcomers into American life as some people claim, but I definitely do not.

Foreign language newspapers can play a great role in helping in the naturalization of our new citizens. Many who come to this country in middle life and immediately start to work will never speak or read English perfectly.

Without being able to learn about this bewildering new land in their own language, they would be separated from America by a thick wall of misunderstanding. Take my own newspaper for example. On our national holidays I think that we print more pictures of Washington and Lincoln, more stories of historic people and events than you will find in any American paper! New citizens are acutely interested in the problems and theories which these holidays celebrate. They have left relatives and friends behind them in troubled countries and so they are eager to read about American traditions of liberty and justice and opportunity, and we print these things, not so much as history, but as news! We treat the Constitution, and freedom of speech and equal justice for all as news, instead of as something won once and for all, a century and a half ago. And it would seem that freedom and justice and human dignity are news—and good news—at this time when so much of the world is in danger of losing these precious privileges.

I often lecture to different groups of new Americans and old ones on this very subject. It is very easy to speak of liberty and justice to people who have for generations suffered slavery and injustice. These words would mean more to them, and have a richer historical substance through personal experience, than they have for Americans.

I remind newcomers from my native country of the bloody demonstrations even within their own lifetime, of many who sacrified their lives for the liberty of Poland and for their own rights as citizens. They understand me because most of them saw their own relatives cut down during street fights during demonstrations for the right to vote. And then I compare their present status, their freedom, their civic rights and their negligence in upholding and taking advantage of these rights. I say to them, "Your fathers fought for the right to vote as a cherished social right. You have received the right to vote, but do you take advantage of it? Are you conscious that your ballot places upon you the responsibility for this country? Do you know that any complaining and criticism of conditions you do not approve of can be laid at your own door?"

Polish psychology does not readily recognize issues at stake during elections here since differences are not so marked as they are abroad where the many parties stand for ideologies of a very definite character.

And even those who come from comparatively happy Polish home backgrounds are amazed by things which Americans take for granted. I have found that Europeans are first impressed by the lack of class distinction they find here. They forgive many disappointments in their new life because they can sit in the same waiting rooms and ride on the same cars as wealthier travellers. It's the Declaration of Independence reduced to everyday human terms! "I ride on plush seats just like millionaires and congressmen!" they say! That proves to them that in

America all men are equal. However, their appreciation of Democracy originates in the knowledge that they actually have an equal start and equal opportunities early in life, which is not the case where class differences existed as social classifications.

The new citizens see America's dangers in a personal way. Many of them have told me that their first great disillusion in this country came when they saw bread in the garbage pails! It fills them with dread and doubt. In the old countries bread is almost sacred. If a piece falls to the floor, a Polish peasant will kiss it before he lays it back on the table. It is this difference in attitudes and customs and ways of thinking that makes the process of changing new citizens into Americans difficult, not differences in language and clothes. That is why I suggest that naturalization should be entrusted as far as possible to Americans of their own background, rather than to native-born workers.

A Polish widow with two children once came to me for help and I managed to get her into the care of a welfare organization. Two weeks later a social worker told me that she would have to take this woman off the rolls. What was wrong? A non-co-operative attitude! I was amazed. "Why do you think that?" I asked. "She tried to push me downstairs!" the worker said. So I decided to go myself and find out the trouble. I took a box of candy to the children, and drank hot tea and talked of this and that, till I arrived at the subject. "Tell me," I said, "Did you really try to push the charity lady downstairs?" "Yes, I did," she told me, "it doesn't matter about my life, but I was not going to let her take my children's blood!" It turned out that the worker had told them she was going to have a blood test taken to make sure that the children did not need treatment! And the woman thought it was the blood-letting she had seen in Poland. In her little village ignorant practitioners sometimes try to cure dying people by cutting a vein in their arm. But of course the American-born social worker who knew nothing of such practices did not think to explain what a blood test really is.

Unfortunately most of our foreign-born citizens are so quick to adopt American ways of dress and habits of living that we don't realize that sometimes this adaptation may be only on the surface. The naturalized Polish boy who learns about America from the movies may pattern his clothes after those worn on the screen, cock his cigarette and hat at a different angle and roll off slang glibly, but in spirit he has not been Americanized. Those who come from his own background and have lived a long time in America and learned to love her traditions and ideals can tell him these things in the right way to reach his understanding. At some periods of our history this lack of like-mindedness might not be so vital, but today with democratic ideas struggling for their life in many lands, we Americans—both native and naturalized—must understand each other and America as never before.

This can be done in one way—the way George Washington believed democracy would be saved—by education! A campaign of education in simple words, which a plain man, and a man with a small English vocabulary can understand. Education as to the exact unprejudiced meaning of all forms of government and how they work out in people's everyday lives. Only by knowing these facts can people protect themselves from subversive ideas. One mistake that those who are interested in Americanization are making is the application of hasty and mass production methods to this very subtle process which requires patience, understanding and above all love and time.

In my own paper, for instance, we are always educating new citizens in the privileges and responsibilities of being an American, by showing them how their own daily lives are affected by living in a democracy. That is all most people are interested in after all—the little circle of their own lives and experience. For instance:—the attitude of the father toward his children; of the policeman toward the man in the street; of the employer toward his employees; all these must undergo a radical change through a process of evolution, which requires first, the destruction of the old and the gradual building up of new attitudes.

Democracy was born of the longing of human hearts for dignity and opportunity and freedom, and it should receive fresh impetus and strength with every boatload of new citizens that lands at Ellis Island. But we waste all their enthusiasm and faith and hope by not taking the trouble to establish a friendly understanding with these new recruits to Democracy. We waste good human material by not trying to use it best. Take the Polish farmer who comes to America for instance. He has an affinity for the soil, and when he has his little earth of his own, he takes root as naturally as a tree. But what do we do? With so much waste land in this great country which in Europe would be tenderly cultivated to the very tops of the mountains, we do not see to it that the naturalized Polish-born citizen has the chance to reach the land. Instead he is lost in the industrial mill where he has no special gifts to give his new country.

You see, I am still a little appalled by the waste of good bread even after twenty years as an American; and the more so by the waste of invaluable human material which properly cared for during the period of adjustment would contribute far more to the ever-growing and ever-changing American nation.

PETER P. YOLLES was born in Poland in 1892 and graduated from high school there and from the Law School of the University of Czernowitz (now Roumania). During World War I he served in the Austrian Army. Immediately upon arriving in the United States in 1921 he entered Columbia University where he received an M.A. degree in Social Sciences in 1925. He continued his

American education with a course in journalism at New York University, concurrently serving as editor of the Polish Morning World (Nowy Swiat). Mr. Yolles is President of the Association of Polish American Publishers and Editors in the United States, and author of several popular novels.

by Joseph Pasternak

BECOMING A MOTION PICTURE PRODUCER was an accident more or less. But I had planned on becoming an American citizen ever since I can remember, long before I came to this country.

When I was a kid running around in a little Hungarian village my elders used to say, "What are you going to be, Joe, when you grow up—a doctor, a farmer, a soldier?" My answer would always be the same, "I'm going to be an American." That gave everyone a big laugh. Occasionally in a more serious mood someone would pat me on the head and say, "Go ahead; you *go* to America." They didn't say, "Go to America and you'll make a lot of money, you'll be famous." They simply said, "Go to America, Joseph, and you'll be free. You'll be somebody there, because in America all men are equal." That's the thing that makes America so great to Europeans!

It's a wonderful feeling, this being an American! Every once in a while I have to go to Europe on business, or I did until about three years ago. One of my greatest hobbies in life is talking to people, so I spoke about my country, America, and the opportunities for happiness it holds for everybody—and I spoke right out! It's a good old American custom, but there are places you can't do that and I was reminded of it in a hurry. I'm sure that my American passport was the only thing that saved me.

Around 1913 my father planned to come to this country with his family. He made us all study English. We couldn't speak it very well, but we could read American papers and books. My early reading wasn't so much American history as Nick Carter stories. Nick was the glamor boy of the 1900's and he was popular in Europe too. Those were fine stories for boys to read. They developed imagination and gave one a liking for adventure. Probably J. Edgar Hoover even read a few of them when he was a boy! They inspired me to read more about America. I used to get books about other Americans as gifts—Washington, Thomas Jefferson, Abraham Lincoln. My father would often read them aloud to the family. But after the war of 1914 was over my father sadly gave up the idea of ever getting to America but said for me to go by myself. He had waited too long.

So in 1921 I landed in Boston alone; then went to Philadelphia where my uncle had been living for twenty-five years. I learned my first lesson in Americanization in Philadelphia too. It was there that I got a job in the same factory where my uncle worked. All of my uncle's friends and acquaintances at home and at work were Hungarians, and they always spoke in Hungarian. One day I asked my uncle why he didn't speak English rather than his native tongue. He said he didn't know the English language. I said, "You've been here twenty-five years, you must know English." His answer was simple, "How could I learn to speak English when all my friends are Hungarians." That day I made a decision that I would only go with people who spoke English and I would speak no other language.

There's a little sequel to that story. About eight years ago the company I worked for at that time sent me back to Hungary to make some motion pictures. The only language I could use there was Hungarian, so I got back the accent which I had lost. Now I'm starting to cure myself all over again.

This brings up a point; something I don't believe a person realizes unless he's been an immigrant to this country himself. Foreigners are very self-conscious—that is, most of the new Americans are—about the language. They go to night schools and they try very hard to master enough English to be able to get along. But when the students go home it's almost like going back to their native countries—for when they step through the door of that flat, or house, or room where they live, they are again thousands of miles away from America and its influences.

The reason for this is very simple for they are caught up by their own nationality groups; those who talk their native tongue. And yet these people are hungry for American talk—talk about American customs and American traditions. They want to be like Americans but their lack of language prevents them from asking questions about the things they want to, and should know. Since my business is one of showmanship it has occurred to me that much good work in Americanization could be done in these night schools and immigrant education groups.

My idea would be to get their interest by telling them stirring stories of the American patriots, like the story of Patrick Henry or the battle of Bunker Hill, or the story of the free press in this country. These are real audience thrillers and it's these liberties our forefathers won that make America so different from any other government in the world.

Democracy is one of those comfortable things that you grow accustomed to without thinking much about, like your wife or your home. We don't spend a lot of time thinking about things we're used to. We take them for granted—the comforts, the companionship, all the things our homes mean to us don't seem so important. But if the marriage goes to pieces and the wife leaves, we realize what we've lost.

I've been trying hard to be a real American for the last

twenty years. But truly, it's surprising how difficult it is for Europeans to understand the close personal feeling we Americans have for our country. We're a part of the government and therefore feel free to criticize it. For example, last year a cousin of mine came over from Europe to see me. We were listening to a radio speech one evening by President Roosevelt. The President made some humorous remark at the beginning of his speech and I laughed. My cousin sat there in stony silence until the speech was over. Then she said, "Why do you laugh at your President, Joe!" I looked at her and tried to explain to her that I thought what he said was funny, but she couldn't understand. She said, "If he were right here in this room speaking to you and you laughed, that would be very very rude. You know that." "No," I replied, "not our President. It would be very rude if he told a joke and we didn't laugh." She can't believe that the head of a country's government would joke.

I think that this proves we are the luckiest people on earth. And if we can keep our sense of humor and don't forget to laugh at ourselves occasionally, and can reason our problems out with plain common sense and keep America the land of opportunity for all her people, I don't believe we need fear dictators will ever get a hold on America.

JOSEPH PASTERNAK was born in Simloul Silvania, Hungary, the son of a poor bookkeeper. In 1920, at the age of nineteen, he arrived in the United States as an immigrant to seek his fortune. His first job was in a Philadelphia belt factory punching holes in leather belts. Then he worked in a poultry market, later as a busboy in a cafeteria. Despite his small wage at this job he was able to save money and he spent it studying to become an actor. He was working in the commissary of Paramount's Long Island studios when he got the opportunity to assist a director in a minor capacity. Since then his rise as a director and producer has become meteoric. He has been responsible for the success of many actors and actresses, chiefly Deanna Durbin and in the past three years has produced eight of Hollywood's most successful productions.

by Dr. Raul d'Eça

DEMOCRACY IS A WORD which has many shades of meaning. It means not only a form of government but a way of living. It means also, as I see it, many great ideals of human conduct and relations which perhaps no country has ever entirely realized. I believe that all Latin American countries cherish the ideals of Democracy, perhaps even more passionately than we ourselves, although they may differ somewhat from the United States in government and political customs. Some of these Latin American countries are in fact virtually dictatorships rather than republics except that you must not confuse Latin American dictatorships with the new European type of dictators. In many of those countries at least 40 per cent of the population cannot either read or write, they live in utter poverty and ignorance. How could these people be expected to inform themselves enough so as to influence their leaders, and decisions? They must trust them to decide their political problems for them. Democracy is a government of reason, intellect, discussion of important questions. Some natives of Brazil in remote districts think that their country is still a monarchy, and that they have an emperor as they did 50 years ago. Nevertheless, in every Latin American country there is an intelligent, well-educated group of people who are willing to sacrifice all for their democratic ideals. Evidently something more than intellectual belief in Democracy is needed, for witness the fall of such countries as France and Holland. That is why I believe that most Latin American countries will not give up their way of living easily. A Guatemalan may not be able to define Democracy but he likes his liberties, and his peaceful relations with his neighbors, and his individuality as a citizen. He prefers this kind of life to any other. I think few South Americans would be happy under a totalitarian government for their temperament and climate and habits would make it insupportable!

The Latin American Republics live together with a minimum of friction because the influence of the United States is, and has always been, since the War of Independence, very great. You will remember that the great South American hero, Bolivar, was a disciple of Jefferson and died clasping a miniature of George Washington, sent to him by the adopted son of Washington. They have tried always to emulate the example of their great neighbor to the north, first by patterning their constitutions after that of the United States and later by adopting in their dealings with each other peaceful means of settling disputes instead of war. This is particularly true in regard to boundary disputes, which elsewhere have always been a source of bitter wars. Brazil offers a good example of this peaceful inclination. With a territory larger than that of the United States, and confining with the three Guianas and all the South American Republics except Chile, she was able to define permanently all her boundaries by arbitration or direct negotiation. The same can be said of the other Latin American nations with only a few exceptions.

I believe that all Latin America is watching the course of the United States in this world crisis, and will be more influenced by our actions than by any threats or persuasions of the totalitarian propaganda. And yet, let us be frank. There is an even more pressing consideration which might sway these Sister Republics in their final stand. And that is the economic consideration—the fundamental problem of making a living, of exchanging their products favorably. We must find ways of establishing closer and mutually profitable economic ties with every one of the other Republics of this hemisphere.

Of course President Roosevelt recognized the truth of this in planning his great economic American cartel, and calling the Havana conference to discuss practical ways and means, but I wonder whether all Americans realize it too, as they must if Democracy is to face the rest of the world resolutely in the Western Hemisphere. It will mean sacrifice of national profit for the sake of our ideals. Yet countries and individuals must realize that—as Benjamin Franklin said, we must hang together or we shall hang separately. The day when we could afford to be isolationists in our personal or national affairs is definitely past. We must think of others' needs and viewpoints or resign ourselves to have all choice taken from us, and some dictator doing our thinking.

The totalitarian propaganda throughout South America in the last few years has been well planned and well executed, the finest music, splendid radio reception, and all remarks framed in perfect Spanish and Portuguese. The United States has not taken the same advantage of radio communication for the purpose of upholding our common ideals, and often the programs that are sent are put into very bad Spanish! Yet, Brazil and the other countries are still loyal, I feel certain, to these common ideals—at least so far.

Latin America is waiting for a clue from the United States that will show her whether we in this country have faith in Democracy to defend it against the world if need be, and to defend it within as well as without. I need not tell you, or any thinking American that we ourselves have not always lived according to the spirit of Democracy, while clinging to its governmental forms. As Mrs. Roosevelt, a very great democrat, has said in her column,

"To people on relief Democracy doesn't amount to a hill of beans!" Without economic Democracy, political Democracy must fail as it has elsewhere.

Yet there is still more opportunity and liberty and hope for the individual here than you will find in any other country in the world today. That is why the Latin American countries still have faith in the United States to become the leader in a plan to balance the needs of its own citizens more equitably, then the needs of the countries of this hemisphere, and last of all the necessities of all the countries in the world. This is the great test of Democracy! It may be also the last chance of Democracy! Can our nation become a leader? Can it step from its isolation and provide a plan for world union? This is, in my opinion, the crucial problem that confronts our generation. Either we find a way of unifying the world along democratic lines or the world is going to be unified, whether we like it or not, by a dictator who will use force, instead of persuasion, to do it. A third alternative is, of course, a complete breakdown of our civilization and a reversion to barbarism.

It is not so important that all men should think alike, nor is it possible that all peoples have the same governmental structure at the same historical moment. But it is important to every man, and to generations to come that people should be able to live in this world secure from fear and aggressions, with their pressing economic needs adjusted. I am not wise enough to make such a plan myself, but this great nation which was once able to frame a constitution like ours in the midst of chaos and doubt and stress, might again rise to her opportunity.

I think that most men, no matter whether they call their countries totalitarian states or democracies, or any other name, would prefer to live at peace instead of at war—like laughter better than sorrow and a calm mind better than anger and hate. The United States with one exception has maintained such an order among her own States for a long while. She is the natural leader in this crisis. If reason and liberty and opportunity and justice for mankind are to survive on earth some nation must assume this leadership. All the Americas look to us! If we have faith enough in Democracy to defend it and to give the world an example of a successful democratic solution of our own economic and social problems we can still justify their faith in us.

RAUL D'EÇA'S birthplace was Aviz, Portugal in 1896. While still a boy he went with an older brother to Brazil where he lived until manhood. Then his desire for further study brought him to the United States. He now holds degrees from a number of American universities, including a Ph.D. from George Washington University, Washington, D. C. For a number of years he was connected with the Pan American Union and now he is Professor of Portuguese and Portuguese and Brazilian

*Literatures at George Washington University. In addi-
tion to this he is considered one of America's outstanding
writers and authorities on Latin American affairs. He
became a U.S. citizen in 1936.*

by Igor Sikorsky

TODAY WE ARE SEEING the results of man's inventiveness and energy turned against his own well being. The airplane which has brought men closer together and increased international trade and prosperity is proving itself the most terrible weapon of destruction the world has ever seen. What can America, from which so many great inventions have come, do to meet this situation?

We must not blame the instrument, but the ill will of mankind which directs it against his neighbor. Ever since the caveman tried to better his way of life by tying a sharp stone to a stick and making a hatchet, the same thing has happened. Some other caveman discovered that this new instrument would not only provide food and firewood but would kill men also. We must think of the airplane today not only as a means of warfare but a strong defense of our peace and security, as well as a faithful servant of human progress. We must be planning for other forms and uses of this great invention, beyond the immediate necessities of a world crisis, so that when dissension dies down we shall be ready to utilize it for the betterment of the world.

America should be the natural leader for such a task. I know, because my career as a designer of aircraft was already well-established when I came here. I have made planes in two lands and I can say honestly that only here will aviation reach its full possibilities for the peaceful expansion of human activities, and for improving people's lives. I felt the difference as soon as I stepped on this shore 20 years ago. Freedom is necessary to the scientist and inventor more even than to other men for great ideas cannot be properly developed in an atmosphere of fear and coercion.

I came here broke, without any special "pull" anywhere. With military aviation being heavily curtailed at that time and commercial flying not yet in existence, I had a difficult time getting started but I did have ideas and hope and determination, and I believed that with these any newcomer could find a chance here. I have even been a little hungry in America. For two years I very seldom spent more than 80 cents a day for food. I have known what it is to seek for work and not find it in America. But there was never a day during the hardest times that I lost hope in my plane or that I did not say aloud, "Thank God I am here, a free man, breathing free air. No man can order what I do! If I fail I can try again!" It takes a naturalized citizen from a less happy country to appreciate what freedom really means. He sees a new world about him, just like a man let out of jail!

If in order to defend the Nation against an invader we should ourselves lose our essential liberties, there would be nothing left worth defending! But we must not get panic-stricken today and fear that we are losing our liberties if the crisis in the world creates the necessity of organizing this Nation for an effective defense. We can take a little discipline without sacrificing any essential rights. A few days ago, when I drove home from Montauk Point the police along the way gave me signals, and orders which I was glad to obey to help keep traffic going. But if they tried to tell me what to teach my children or how I should worship, that would be a different matter. We must not confuse these two coercions at this time. We have to bring order into our life to prepare quickly for our defense, but as long as the government doesn't come into my home and my family and religion, does not interfere with legitimate work and activities—and as long as I can climb on a soap box and say what I please even to criticizing the Government, why then, America is still America!

I think that I can speak about Democracy with conviction for I have lived in other countries. I have seen the alternative, and I want my children and myself to live in this country which is still the land of freedom and

71

opportunity, in which Democracy is a real active principle and tradition, not just a name.

How can Americans, native or naturalized, contribute individually and personally toward making democracy effective—how can we strengthen our spiritual defenses? This is a vast subject. It includes the control of difficulties caused by the present crisis and it also includes problems which humanity has had to face for many centuries. The great problems that are shaking the structure of civilization today are perhaps beyond the solution of the individual man, but he can contribute something toward their solution, in his own field—toward the improvement of the life of his own time.

Let's take my own field for example. The airplane is the fastest and, in many respects, the most efficient method of transportation. It can carry government officials or mail several times faster than other methods of travel. It can bring quick relief carrying doctors, medical supplies, food, and so forth, to a community stricken by some disaster. But the plane can also bring disaster by carrying bombs, fire and destruction, and it is not the plane, and usually not even the pilot who chooses the mission on his flight. I am confident that good will and common sense will guide this Nation and its leaders in designating missions to our aircraft. As long as this is the case, airplanes will remain the best protection of our land, our freedom and our homes, from invasion, as well as a very vital factor contributing to the peaceful progress and well-being of our people. One of the worst disasters of war is that it interrupts progress and turns men's efforts from creative work for better lives for man, to plans for death and destruction. Think how far we might have advanced in civilization and high living standards if our invention and effort had not been continually sidetracked by some war! We must not allow this to continue. While at present the question of aircraft for national defense is urgent and must be given serious attention, of still greater and permanent importance is the creation of such types of aircraft which would be of direct service to the average American of modest means. Think what an improvement it would make in the lives of workers if they could fly in their own planes from their places of business to homes in uncrowded, healthful places many miles away! With small aircraft that can start and descend anywhere and cost no more than an average automobile there need be no more slums or crowded cities! Really, this is no more fantastic than the first plan to bring automobiles into our everyday lives. But how can it be done? Airplanes have required big landing fields. I have great hope in the direct lift type of aircraft. With propellers at the top it can start from a small space, and land on an equally small one. That means that it can reach undeveloped land where even an automobile can't go now. America is still not nearly developed. There are plenty of places that are inaccessible now where good land can be bought for $5 an acre. With mass production methods

73

the cost of a small private plane might be brought within the reach of the man with a small salary.

I believe that it is practical and I am conducting test flights in a small flying machine of that type at the present time. The modest flights that have already been made leave no doubt as to the possibilities connected with such type of aircraft.

This is typically a democratic goal in a time when so much of the world seems bent on slaughter. America has no territorial ambitions, no other aim than better living for its people and peaceful relations with its neighbors. That is why I say that a new inexpensive form of transportation such as I have outlined could only come to fruition in America and in no other country in the world. The automobile made modern America what it is today. Popularized flying may make the America of the future. I see no reason to lose this faith because of the seeming failure of Democracy in some European countries. Totalitarianism need not necessarily be shrewd and clever and democracy weak and inefficient. Within the framework of our own national institutions and our own American way of life, we can and must organize our spiritual strength and produce the material equipment that would protect permanently our Land, freedom and traditions.

IGOR SIKORSKY was born in Kiev, Russia, in 1889 and in 1909 he became active in aviation and between that date and 1912 designed and built two helicopters, two air-driven sleighs and six different types of airplanes. In the following year, Sikorsky completed and successfully flight-tested the first large multi-motored airplane in the world. After the Revolution of 1917, he came to the United States, and in 1923 organized the first aircraft company bearing his name. Since then Sikorsky has been one of the world's foremost designers and builders of planes, and he is especially known for his development of the flying clipper ship. In 1928 he became a citizen of the United States.

by Louis Adamic

WHAT STORY COULD BE GREATER than the story of the meeting on this continent of peoples from sixty different backgrounds! Eighty-five years ago Walt Whitman said of America, "This is not a nation, but a teaming of nations!" I believe firmly that the consciousness of our all-inclusive national story by all Americans would be an inspiration for greater unity and oneness of purpose. In direct contrast to the vicious nonsense about pure races, we should glorify and exploit the fact that America is and always has been a country of many strains drawn from all over the world—and we should make this diversity the basis of a culture and civilization greater than any the world has ever known.

In a time of world crisis like this we Americans must have more than a passive faith in our institutions and our past. We need an enthusiasm, a positive plan for the future.

I'd say that the way to do that is to stop a moment, here today, and think of what we have here on this continent, in this vast and beautiful country and first of all realize, perhaps that we have here something called the American Dream which was founded on a dream. Men brought this dream here from many lands. Many were Americans before they came. They looked for a common ground on which to stand with other men in an atmosphere of freedom. They brought with them what we know now as America.

To me Americanism is nobody's monopoly, but a happy concentration of some of the best aspirations of humanity almost everywhere. As it seems to me, Americanism is the highest body of idealism in the world today—a movement away from primitive racism, fear and hard instincts toward freedom, creativeness, a universal culture. Most of our immigrants of the last century were escaping from oppression of some kind, either political or economic. To them, as to the Pilgrims, America was a refuge, a chance for a better life. She offered it to them herself.

I am referring not to the glittering promises of the agents sent abroad by American industrialists to recruit workers, but to the lines engraved fifty-four years ago on the base of the Statute of Liberty! I wonder whether most Americans know that they are there.

"Give me your tired, your poor
　Your huddled masses yearning to breathe free

The wretched refuse of your teeming shore
Send these, the homeless, the tempest tossed to me
I lift my lamp beside the golden door."

The economic need of men for America's labor short-
age which led this country to open her doors to the
world no longer exists. The point I want to make is that
the people who came to this country by way of Ellis
Island as well as those who came by Plymouth Rock and
Jamestown were led not merely by the desire for material betterment but by a great common hope. They were
breaking away from the heavy paths of the old world
and were looking to the future . . . to the possibility of
self-realization of creativeness, of growth and human
worth. A common emotion, faith, yearning, made a nation
out of people from many lands—if we are to stay a nation
we must again share this common emotion. We must
make alive again the motives that brought us together
and turn them into ties strong enough to hold us together.

There are twenty-five hundred foreign born Americans
in "Who's Who in America," some of our greatest scientists, artists, musicians, educators. And these are not the
only foreign-born who have made America great. Most
of the newcomers in the last hundred years went into
hard manual labor when they came, building, digging,
grubbing, carrying burdens—with the result that now
there is hardly a building you see, or a bridge or a mile
of railroad or highway that is not in part a result of their

labor! There are no statues to these new Americans. Present-day America itself is their creation!

There are today about ten million Irish-Americans, between fifteen and twenty millions of German background, about five million who stem from Italy, four million from Scandinavia, and so on. We have four and a half million Jews who come or stem from many countries. I sometimes think that these new Americans represent the liberty-loving elements in their original countries and that one way to explain the European tragedy of today is that immigration to America drained Europe of those who have the will to defend their freedoms.

It is true that some of us who came here have not been true to ourselves, to the impulse that brought us here. Much is wrong here, as in Europe. In Europe there is now another dream—the dream of personal power held by so-called Men of Destiny. It's a nightmare, tumbling the Old World and its cultures into ruin. If we are going to defend democracy in America, we must know clearly just how much democracy we have to defend. We need to take stock of our human resources both new and old stock American alike. We are facing difficult times, and we'll need everything we've got. But I believe that this period is in a way a testing time for us. This period of crisis is really a fresh opportunity for us.

Somewhere along our way, in our hurry to build great cities, and industries, we have almost lost sight of the dream that brought us here, all of us from Jamestown to

Ellis Island. Now in these fateful months we watch what is happening elsewhere in the world and we are appalled. But to be appalled is no answer to anything! We must summon and organize the initial emotion that brought us here—that made our knees sink on the hard rocks at Plymouth and that brought tears to our eyes when we passed the Statue of Liberty.

It is not too late to save the American dream and make Democracy a practical program of life for all of our people as well as an ideal. On the contrary, this is our moment! This is our great chance to begin to become a homogeneous people, to begin to interlace our complicated past into a unified pattern and culture. Now we can do things. Now our situation is clearer than ever before. This crisis has made us suddenly aware of our weakness as a country—weakness which the dictators of the totalitarian countries are counting on to help them defeat the democracies.

When this country was formed there were people—Jefferson among them—who believed that the hope of the world was here. They were probably right. The failure of America to harness the dreams of its past into the processes of its life is one of the greatest wastes of human resources this age has known. Into no country ever was so much of the best of human yearnings poured.

Awareness is the first step in a practical plan of action. We need to take stock of our human resources, embark upon self-appraisal, self-discovery and self-criticism, before we can come into our heritage of courageous co-operative living. Before us is the necessity of a tremendous effort if we are not to be swallowed by the nightmare of the Old World. We need, each of us, to train ourselves to be interested in a man because he is different and may have something from his own background to offer us personally. We need to get acquainted with our fellow Americans of other strains than our own, and make opportunities to meet with them and discuss our ideas and discover theirs. We need to avoid the language of intolerance which is so un-American, the derogatory nick-names for new immigrant groups, Hunkies and Kikes and Greasers and Chinks, the suspicions that now seem to follow a man because we can't pronounce his name. If we begin to think unity and strive for unity we will, I think, begin to find ourselves bound by the common emotions and purposes which made America in the beginning and which can still, and I am sure *will*, create a civilization and culture greater than any the world has ever known.

LOUIS ADAMIC was born in 1899 of peasant parents in the province of Carniola, now part of Yugoslavia. He came to the United States as an immigrant boy of fourteen and became an American citizen in 1918 while at Camp Beauregard, Louisiana as a soldier in the U.S. Army. He has visited every state in the Union, has been a factory worker, steel worker, sailor, harbor pilot's assistant and worked in many other fields. Mr. Adamic is the author of some seven books, the best known of which is probably "The Native's Return" which described a brief return to his native land. His most recent book "From Many Lands" is the foremost study of the foreign-born American.

★ 13 ★

by Senator Robert F. Wagner

IN ONE EUROPEAN DEMOCRACY after another, failure to solve economic problems has destroyed the faith of the common man in a system of free enterprise. Democracy, after all, means much more than going through the motions of popular government. It is an instrument to foster life, liberty and the pursuit of happiness by the people at large in their daily working lives. Men do not struggle to defend something they do not have and to which they cannot aspire. Armaments are essential, of course, to defend our land and our institutions against invasion by any combination of hostile powers. But my point is, democracy cannot be defended by armaments alone.

The social legislation which safeguards economic freedom in America and helps uphold a man's faith and hope in the democratic way of life as it applies practically to himself and his family, is one of our strongest national defenses. There was a time, not so long ago, when most of us tended to take for granted that the democratic way of life would thrive and extend its blessings to every corner of the earth. Today the democratic way is very much on the defensive. There are new forces abroad in the world—Fascism and Communism—thriving on social discontent and economic privation, offering a fanciful security for the sacrifice of human rights. These forces have found other democracies, bewildered, disillusioned, defenseless—and we know what has happened—dictatorship!

The steady retreat of democracy overseas has been paralleled by the steady advance of democracy in America, for the very reason that we have taken to heart the very lesson I am stressing. We have made great gains in projecting the ideals of freedom and equality of opportunity into every phase of our economic life. These gains are an important part of the ramparts we watch today.

Our social reforms have by no means been premature. There have been times in our history when forward-looking men and women feared that their new measures were too early. Today our chief concern is whether we are not too late—too late to save our economic system after years of neglect. Insecurity and social maladjustment are enemies within our gates. In the present state of world affairs, we can no more afford to adopt a half-hearted policy of appeasement toward them than toward a potential invading foe.

Our recent social legislation had its roots deep in the American tradition of individual dignity and mutual service. It extends to the industrial problems of the 20th Century the faith in human values that is so fundamental in our national thinking. But we must not make the mistake of supposing that there is anything unique in our social and labor legislation. Slum clearance, for example, has been an accepted public responsibility in Great Britain and the Scandinavian countries for many years. And as for disputes over labor's right to organize, that right is so generally recognized in these countries that no laws were needed to guarantee its enforcement.

Labor union is democracy in action. It is to the worker what the corporation is to the businessman, and what the marketing co-operative is to the farmer. Labor wants just about what all Americans want—neither more nor less. His right to organize and to bargain collectively with his employer is his essential protection against economic exploitation and—in some instances—denial of political rights and civil liberties. I can conceive of nothing more alien to the American way of life than the denial of industrial freedom. And I say there is no more splendid vindication of democracy than the now-established practice of giving workers the chance to select their own representatives by secret ballot. Of course, we are always striving for greater industrial peace, but that can be done most successfully, experience shows, by recognition of the rights of workers as free men. If we wiped out labor unions and employers' associations, and settled all employer-employee disputes by government decree, there would perhaps be no more labor troubles, but there would also be no more democracy in America. We will have adopted the dogmas of the totalitarian states—forced labor and denial of the employer's property rights, the inevitable consequences of dictatorship.

Do you realize that many of the social reforms we have been talking about, and now part of our normal peacetime economy, were established as emergency measures during the World War? They proved necessary to make industry and labor both function more efficiently! Today instead of having to blunder until we work out a defense program, we have labor standards already established, a United States Employment Service ready to fit men to jobs, collective bargaining and labor mediation to reduce the danger of delays through industrial disputes, a housing authority to help provide shelter for expanding industrial areas, and many other instruments we needed and used for national defense during the last war.

I would say there are at least four answers to the suggestion that labor standards must be modified in the interest of national defense. The first is this. The original 40-hour week law in France was a 40-hour week for factories as well as for their workers. There is nothing in our labor laws to hinder American factories from operating 24 hours a day, and an increasing number of our factories are in fact operating on three shifts. The second answer is that our factories are not hindered by law from providing a longer work-week for their employees if they pay them time-and-a-half for overtime for the extra hours. The third answer lies in our unemployment situation. Five million workers are registered in the United States Employment Offices for all types of jobs, including skilled labor needed for national defense. We must find and give work to these unemployed millions before we begin to work present employees overtime.

The final answer is that experience here and in Great Britain proves conclusively that long hours of labor do not necessarily result in increased production of goods. During the last war, the Chief of Ordnance of the United States Army made this statement: "Industrial history proves that fair working conditions and a proper wage-scale are essential to high production."

For many decades America has looked to its foreign-born to do its hardest and most poorly paid work, and yet these new citizens sometimes have a keener appreciation of our democracy and its rights and privileges than many of our native-born. Perhaps the answer is that those born under a foreign rule with memories of another way of life do not take the privileges and freedoms of democracy lightly or for granted. They came here—they left their homes, families, familiar surroundings—because they believed that democracy would really provide freedom and opportunity for them and their children. They think of freedom not merely as a word in a patriotic vocabulary but as something to cherish—to struggle for—to fight for and defend—and if need be, to die for! It is not often realized that one out of every three persons in our population today is foreign-born or has a foreign-born parent. Only in a democracy has it been possible for those many races and creeds to live and work in peace, and contribute their full measure toward the common goal of national greatness. Only through renewed devotion to that democratic ideal, can we maintain the national unity which is so essential to the national defense.

ROBERT F. WAGNER was born in Nastatten, Hesse-Nassau, Germany in 1877 and came to the United States in his early childhood. He attended schools in New York City where he began his own law practice and entered politics. In 1914 he became Lt.-Governor of New York and from 1919 until 1926 was Justice of the Supreme Court of N. Y. Since 1927 he has been U.S. Senator from New York. Much important legislation has been introduced by Senator Wagner, chiefly the National Recovery Act, and the Social Security Act.

by William Knudsen

ONLY DEMOCRACY GIVES a man the opportunity to make as much or as little of himself as he wishes. That's the difference in my mind between Democracy and Totalitarianism . . . the difference between centralization and decentralization, the State and the individual. My own mental picture of Democracy shows a country, or a city, a community or factory, a farm or a simple home where justice, care for the sick or weak, and the greatest good for all is obtained with the greatest amount of individual action possible.

There were five hundred who came over here on my boat forty-one years ago. I don't know what became of the four hundred and ninety-nine others, but I've no doubt that many of them did well over here, and I'd be willing to wager that not one of them starved. America treated each of us as we treated America, and I think it's pretty much the same way today. If you want work and will hustle out and take what you can get and not sit around and wait for a fancy job to be brought to you, you can still find plenty of opportunities here and now.

Democracy *is* a going concern. I've read a lot of articles and books that we're headed for ruin, that we've come to the end of our road—that the economic system we've developed can't take care of all our workers, that we've got no more frontiers. My answer is just this; I don't believe a word of it. Not a word! I know that it isn't so! Maybe I've been lucky, but when I look at executives today every man of them came up from the bench the same as I did. You can't be too choosy though! It's easier to blame the economic system than yourself if you haven't got a job.

When I started here I didn't ask for the kind of work I wanted—I merely asked for work. There's always something to be done. In forty-one years I've been out of work just eight months, and six of them I was sick. In other words I believe that work is the cure for the imaginary ills of our present status and that the old saying, "boosting the sweat of our brow" is still good medicine.

I never questioned whether I was born American or an American with a hyphen from the day I landed. I never thought whether I was American or Danish. Maybe some do. I didn't. I was too busy. Now and then I was called a squarehead. But that didn't hurt me! Some people take their country with them wherever they go, like the character in Mark Twain, but to my way of thinking those who come to the United States bring faith in America with them, the love of freedom, and self-expression that brought people over from the first. That's the source of America's strength. It's the only country in the world that is constantly being reborn. The strongest and most forward-looking men and women in any country are the pioneers who leave home for new fields. America is made up of those.

Yet I think that Americans take their Democracy for granted, the way we take light and air and life for granted. Not because they are indifferent but because it is a part of them, a part of their flesh and blood. We don't feel the need of discussing and exclaiming over the fact that we have two arms and two legs. We accept them as natural. But that doesn't mean that we would be willing to do without them. We don't need to supercharge patriotism in America, but we can be sure that it will be there if it's needed. America is the most emotional country in the world. When people here are told about famines or disasters or war and destruction in other parts of the world what happens? The children in the little villages start saving their pennies to help. The women in farmhouses and cabins and the homes of workers stop in the midst of their housework to knit socks. In what other country would you find people doing such things for strangers? Evidently the enemies of Democracy are counting on our unmixed racial strains as a weakness which they can use to destroy us.

I have often been asked if I see danger in the fact that we are all immigrants at one time or another. I do not. Perhaps some of the first generation in this country have a little difficulty mixing, but the second and third generations are born Americans. Let me tell you a little story. . . . I worked once in a machine shop where most of the workers were Hungarians. One day I showed a businessman through the shop and he remarked that he saw our workmen were all "Hunkies!" Five years later the same man visited the shop again, and walked through the machine room. "Why," he exclaimed, "what have you done with your Hunkies?" I pointed to the men who were working. . . . "Here they are," I said, "only now they have become Americans!" They did not look like immigrants now. They were eating better food, wearing better clothes, living according to American standards of living, and they looked no different from any American working men. There wasn't any difference!

Many of our immigrants never learn English well enough to understand what Democracy has done and is doing for them, and so they were easy subjects for propaganda in their own native tongue, on the radio or in their group newspapers, but I think this is gradually taking care of itself. The children do much to explain American ways and institutions to their elders. Young people are quick to pick up language, clothes, customs of America. I thought that I spoke English when I arrived from Denmark, but when I opened my mouth strange sounds came out of it! I had no money for lessons so I talked to children, and every night after work I sat on the stoop of my boarding house and talked to the children on my street. Children use the simplest, most direct speech in the world. So I learned English quickly. Perhaps that is one reason why I have always felt so at home.

I don't think I write as I do because of anything I've done or any success I've made in this country. The best thing I have gotten from America that counts is an American family. My wife was born in Buffalo, of German ancestry. Three of my children are married. One daughter married a boy of Dutch ancestry, my son married a girl of Scotch ancestry, and another daughter a boy of Canadian background. I have three grandchildren! America is a country of families—that's why I'm not afraid for its internal security. The strength or weakness of every country is in its families. I don't think that wealth even counts for so much to a pioneering people. Fortunes come and go in America, they seldom last more than a generation or two. I've made money and I didn't love America more.

Immigrant is just another name for pioneer. We all came here to find independence and self-expression as much as wealth. In the old days the Vikings went forth and sold their shield and sword and battle axe to the service of other men, and were loyal to the men who treated them fairly and squarely. America treats its people decently, protects their constitutional guarantees, gives them a chance to make a living and educate their children, all Americans, whether they're native or foreign-born, will treat America decently in turn.

The American people as I know them will consent to any sacrifice they think is needed to preserve our Democracy, but they wouldn't put up a minute with pomp and pretensions. Americans would laugh the pretensions of dictatorship out of countenance. I never fail to get a kick out of coming back to the United States and seeing the pilot coming aboard at Sandy Hook. No fuss, no uniforms, no salutes. A man dressed in a slouch hat with a cigar in his mouth climbs the ladder. A short greeting on the bridge. He goes, Bing! Bing! and off we go. That's America as I see it, and may God help us to always keep it so!

WILLIAM S. KNUDSEN was born in Denmark and came to America at the age of twenty. On his arrival here he worked in New York shipyards and in the Erie Railroad shops, studying English and other subjects in the evening. Later he was employed at the Ford Motor Company on the assembly lines where he acquired great skill as an engineer and mechanic. After leaving the Ford Company he was an executive of several other automotive companies before joining the General Motors Cor-

poration, where he later became President. Mr. Knudsen recently took leave of absence from this position to become Director of the Industrial Production Division of our National Defense Program.

by Tony Sarg

I HAVE FOUND that laughter is a universal language. A joke is one thing that doesn't spoil with age. Some of my puppets tell funny stories from the Arabian Nights and they bring the same bursts of laughter today as they did two thousand years ago, and people of all nations laugh at the same things. When I was a schoolboy in Frankfort I kept my friends doubled up with the caricatures of my teachers I drew for them. American children think such caricatures are funny too. That love of laughter brought to our shores from every land is intensified in America until our sense of humor has become one of our most striking national characteristics. We love those who can make us laugh.

Perhaps that explains why I have had none of the struggles which so many immigrants seem to experience in establishing themselves for I have certainly been very fortunate in America. When I came here from London in 1915 I brought fully a hundred letters of introduction to various people who might help me get started, but the day after I arrived I got an order to illustrate a story for a leading periodical and it brought so much business that I never did have to present any of those letters.

I know that no matter how fantastic the idea I had I have always found an American businessman who was glad to listen to it, and take a chance on helping get it started. The children of Europe have known and loved these little figures animated by strings for five hundred years but they were almost unknown in America when I came here. Americans are generous and hospitable to new ideas.

To artists at least an atmosphere of freedom is an essential to producing good work. To me certainly.—The secret of success and happiness has always been to be able to do the thing I most like to do in life for nobody really does a good job unless he loves doing it—I was brought up as a little boy with many small duties.—Even at the age of six my father woke me up every morning at six to feed some chickens on the farm. I hated this early job, but soon I devised a spring pulley from my bedroom window to open the chicken coop. Instead of getting up I just pulled a string and the chickens came out of the coop and ate their breakfast which I had put there the evening before. That started things for me and I have been pulling strings for myself ever since—on puppets, mostly.

It is too soon to predict what effect regimentation and the education of whole populations to new ideas may have upon the arts. A caricaturist, for instance, is an artist with a message, but even this form of art would probably flourish better in a democracy where people are able to laugh at themselves as well as at those who disagree with them. I believe that with the confusion and change abroad many good European artists will meet here on this soil, and that America may thus really preserve civilization and art through this troubled epoch.

Frankly I don't share the forebodings of some Americans who fear that democracy is in danger in America as it is in so many other countries. I thoroughly believe that we should be ready to defend our way of life whenever it is necessary, but I think that there is one good reason why Americans will never accept any form of dictatorship.

We have spoken of that reason already—our American sense of humor! In governments without this saving national grace of laughter and self-ridicule the forms and ceremonies that go with dictatorship would appeal to Americans' love of the ridiculous. You may remember the old Keystone comedies which owed their popularity to the delight of the audience in seeing a cocky, pompous policeman discomfited by a piece of custard pie! Can you imagine an average American husband whose wife has a struggle to get him to buy a new suit or wear his tuxedo once a year being told to wear a shirt of some especial

color? Can you picture an American businessman saying "Heil Anybody!" before he answers his telephone?
Can you imagine any American making curious gestures
and mystic motions when they meet each other on the
street? Why, America and particularly we cartoonists
would laugh a dictator out of countenance at the first
symptom of solemn pompousness!

Other democracies have not been able to defend themselves by laughter because they were too close to each
other. Even in America we cannot laugh at the situation
abroad for too many of our people have come from
Europe within one or two generations. They are anxious
over the situation of relatives and friends and still cherish
the memory of the towns and scenes they have come
from. This freedom of self-criticism which goes with the
democratic idea and does not exempt any American from
ridicule and fun-poking is our greatest safeguard. When
the time comes when we cannot joke about one of our
public men, or kid our leaders, *then* Democracy will be
in danger.

An important question today is how America might
present democracy in a vital way to our children. Perhaps
my experience with marionettes may provide an answer.
Enthusiasm and emotion is necessary and I have found
that children respond enthusiastically to any kind of art
which they help create, and share. That is why they
love puppet shows. Children call on their own powers
of imagination. I discovered how much every child in

the audience does to endow my little wooden figures with life when I stepped out from behind the curtain after one performance to take a bow. A shriek of surprise and fright went up as if they saw a giant!

Perhaps freedom, like art, must have enthusiasm and emotion to survive. And children, and grown-up children will respond with all their hearts if they are given a personal part to play in democracy and a creative job to do for America—which demands more of them than singing the national anthem.

TONY SARG was born in Guatemala in 1882 but grew up, and received his education in Germany. He was a German army officer until 1905 when he began his career as an illustrator in London. In 1915 Mr. Sarg came to the United States and was naturalized in 1921. He is known for his many illustrated books, mainly for children, and for the marionettes with which he has become identified internationally.

by Judge Ferdinand Pecora

I CAME TO THIS COUNTRY when I was five years old and have never stepped from American soil since then. Several times in former years I have been on the point of visiting my native land but I have had a rather busy life and something always intervened to prevent it. Today, however, I doubt whether any citizen of a democracy with such passionate convictions as I have expressed whenever I have had the opportunity, would be welcomed by a totalitarian government.

I have expressed these views in no uncertain terms for it is certainly a time for plain and honest speech. Already we may have waited too long to discuss frankly our American institutions among ourselves and review their relation to the present times. Democracy must grow to remain democratic. If we ever come to regard it as a completed system of government, as something static and definitive, instead of plastic, then it is no longer democracy. And the natural way of growth and safety for a system which depends upon the will of free men is through discussion and education.

For a hundred and fifty years before the Constitution was written, human beings from every land had been bringing to these shores the passionate desire for civil and religious freedom, and for that equality of opportunity and justice which they were denied in their own countries. There was never a nation in the history of the world into the making of which so much human aspiration and yearning were poured! From the sharing of these intense desires, and from a century-and-a-half of discussion about men's rights and liberties, came slowly and painfully, with many temporary recessions, the formulation of the democratic creed. A principle of government born of so much effort, struggle, hope and faith is surely something that we should often re-examine, to make sure that it is working as it was intended for the continual betterment of all our people.

Some Americans accept their rights and privileges too matter-of-factly perhaps, but I also think that many Americans, including some of the eight million naturalized citizens now in our country—have not adequately learned to understand these rights and privileges and responsibilities, and all of their implications. That is one of the reasons why we find in our large cities many sections populated almost wholly by Old World racial groups who follow still the Old World ways and customs of life. I know naturalized citizens who have made their way to success in America from a boyhood of poverty, but yet run their business and treat employees according to Old World traditions and standards, as though they had ever heard of Democracy.

Education in the meaning and significance of democracy is an ideal way to safeguard Democracy. Unfortunately, some of our naturalized citizens never learn our language well enough to really understand America; but their children who attend our public schools are not likely to present that problem. Another way to democratic progress, of course, is through modification of our laws, to adapt them to conditions as they arise.

As a lifelong student of laws, I believe that we can adjust the principles of Democracy to violent world upheaval and economic bewilderment through the making of new laws speedily enough to protect us from the disasters that have befallen free men in other parts of the world. Everywhere conditions of life are changing rapidly. The old legal systems which protected men's rights and liberties in Seventeen Hundred and Eighty are no longer sufficient. Democracy must widen the scope of its guarantees to meet new pressures and problems. Fortunately our foresighted founding fathers wrote all the necessary machinery for governmental growth into the Constitution. Violence may accompany crisis and change in other less flexible systems. Only Democracy is planned for peaceful change.

In 1912 I became a member of the National Progressive or Bull Moose Party, and was one of its officers during its life. I remember hearing the late Theodore Roosevelt say during his Presidential Campaign in 1912, "If Democracy is to mean the happiness and contentment its founders intended for all Americans, *we must pass prosperity around.*" A year later the income tax law was enacted; and since then we have been adopting other laws designed to pass prosperity around a little more equitably among all Americans. It is sometimes a slow process, and often it loses ground. But over the years we steadily advance through our laws toward the better realization of the freedoms and opportunities which are the ideals of Democracy. We advance.

Individual initiative, the hope of advancement through one's own efforts—these elements seem to me fundamentals of progress in the American spirit. The Capitalistic system may have its faults, but it is still better fitted to human nature than any other yet devised. Progress, prosperity, are not matters of national resources alone. Other nations have resources equal to America's, yet without the advantages of equality of opportunity and the right of private property, their people appear to lack the vital urge that makes for better standards of living.

If men wish to preserve our tradition of equality of opportunity for all, they must either be educated to pass prosperity around voluntarily, or they must be constrained to do so by laws which make for social and economic justice. Paradoxically speaking, men are learning to be unselfish through reasons of self-interest in order to retain the right of private property. But laws themselves come as the result of public opinion and so it sometimes goes back to the question of hastening the processes of education. Other ideologies resort to campaigns of propaganda. Yet that seems foreign to the American way.

That is another paradox of democracy,—that its own rights and privileges can be used to do it harm. In a recent decision I called attention to this. The clipping from the New York Law Journal quotes "far better it is to preserve the right freely to debate political issues unhampered even with the abuses which frequently attend its exercise than to limit it at the possible loss of our Constitutional liberties."

And yet, it is to my mind a grave question whether organizations which represent ideologies hostile to American democracy, or which are controlled from lands inimical to America, should be permitted to acquire the legal status of a political party with all the privileges and immunities which our laws confer upon political parties. As one who was born on foreign soil, but who has transplanted his roots to America and enjoyed the great blessings of its free institutions, I cherish with all my soul its inestimable rights of freedom of speech, freedom of the press, freedom of conscience, and equality before the law. These liberties have made America truly great. They are indispensable to the sound development of man's dignity and happiness. But I am troubled at the possibility that their very exercise by alien-minded men and parties may ultimately bring about the actual destruction of these precious rights. This is a matter worthy of the earnest attention, not only of our legislatures, but, of all thoughtful democracy-loving Americans.

FERDINAND PECORA was born in Nicosia, Italy in 1882 and when he was five he came to the United States with his family. He attended The College of the City of New York, and New York Law School. From 1918 until 1930 he was active as Assistant District Attorney of New York. In 1930 he became Counsel for the U.S. Senate Committee on Banking and Currency and afterwards became one of the original members of the Securities and Exchange Commission, set up by President Roosevelt. He resigned from this position in 1935 to accept the Governor's appointment as Justice of the Supreme Court of New York State.

by Dr. Ales Hrdlička

IT IS A VERY TRYING THING to be an anthropologist today and witness the civilization of whole nations, which it took so many centuries to attain, being squandered. Nevertheless, Man's history shows us there is no reason to despair of his further progress and of his future. The ultimate effect upon man's evolution of the world's present troubles will not be pronounced. Nature, including all that we understand under this term, repairs the ravages of war, famine and other great disasters in a remarkably short time. During and after the Thirty Years' War, and again during and after the World War, millions of people perished of wounds, disease or starvation. In Russia, which from 1914 to 1924 suffered so that the stature and even the size of the head of the people in some regions were affected, today, only a generation later, all the measurements are once more normal and the population in every respect is forging forward. Time after time plagues and wars in the Middle Ages reduced the population of European countries to half their size, but nature repaired the loss within a few generations.

Of course, this is taking the long view of ˜cience. We, who must live in our little contemporary moment of history would not be recompensed for the loss of our liberties, for example, by the knowledge that there may be no lasting set-back to human evolution! A large part of the human world is in one of the most destructive eruptions of all time and the rest is in growing danger, danger to its possessions, to its organization, to all the civic achievements for which it has long labored and which it holds dear. With all other Americans, the scientist must rise from his seclusion, and the student come down from his tower to consider the problems of the moment.

It seems to me that one of the major problems before the American people today is that of the alien, the stranger in the family. But my definition of an alien would be broader than usual; it would be a man or woman who has not yet learned to know and appreciate America, who, regardless of papers, has not grown into one with the American people, whose prime interests and sympathies, from ignorance or selfish reasons, are still with governments and things not American.

The dire examples of countries that have already succumbed have shown that a proportion of the unassimilated foreign elements may contribute a serious internal peril at a time when unity is most needed, as it is in the present world crisis. For it is a fact that some proportion of such unassimilated elements remains more subservient to the country of its origin than to that of its adoption. America is now truly in a critical position; more dangerous position than perhaps as yet is generally appreciated, for its whole future is staked on liberal government and institutions, and on freedom in commercial relations. It surely harbors among its aliens, with the great majority of good and true, some disloyal elements, and the problem is how to safeguard the country against these individuals.

The first and one of the most important steps in Americanization, in my opinion, is to counteract the prejudice against the immigrant and foreign-born, simply because they are such. This prejudice of course is natural and others in this forum feel the same way about this problem. The American, too, would meet with it if he went to live in another country. It is encountered by many a bridegroom or bride coming into a new family. It is based on a number of deep-set feelings—the dislike of what one is not used to, the fear of unpleasant behaviors, the hidden apprehension of competition; but the chief source of all of this is lack of acquaintance. And acquaintance with a foreigner is difficult. He speaks at best but poor English, has other habits, other food, and other associations. He must prove himself before being accepted. And meanwhile he is neglected, often abused, and generally distrusted. In times like the present a general distrust of our foreign-born might become actually dangerous to the national endeavors.

A favorite device for fostering racial intolerance today seems to be through the theory advanced by some governments that their people are inherently superior to others, and must not risk contamination by mixing with inferior strains. Neither anthropology nor psychology has ever been able to find any basic difference in the various subdivisions of the White stock; and as the historical and ample other evidence shows, there is not a single pure nationalistic or geographic group among the White people. Moreover, while there are prevalent differences in color, stature, or form of the head, and even in behavior, all these are differences of secondary nature and have no bearing on the intellectual endowments or character standards of the various groups. It is well known that there is no sameness in such features even in the same families, yet how absurd it would seem to every father and mother if anyone would want to grade their children according to such differences. And a nation is only a large family. People differ in their habits and in their enlightenment, but these are environmental differences; the average endowments and capacities in normal contingents of the great White stock are, it is now known definitely, much the same.

With human races at large it is as though at the beginning of mankind, five or six different groups of people started out on the long hard road to civilization in so many different directions. Some found the way more propitious and went ahead faster. Others encountered bogs and crags and got belated. But among the Whites there are not any seriously belated. May the teachers and the children in our schools and colleges learn this truth, and a great deal toward the lightening of the problem of the alien shall have been accomplished.

In my opinion naturalization helps greatly to solve the problem of the alien in America—the stranger in the family as we have called him. For one thing, the alien who becomes a citizen must be able to use the English language to some extent, and must pass examinations which show that he has reached some understanding of our democratic institutions and responsibilities. Yet there are still three and one-half million people in America today who as yet have not become citizens. The reasons, as I had ample personal opportunities to learn, are insufficient knowledge of English, fear of the needed examinations, not intending to stay in this country, or a simple neglect. The learning of the language came harder to some of the immigrants, especially to those who were older. Others lived for years among their own kind where English was not needed; there were too few facilities for adults to learn properly, and hard labor made the additional effort for study of the language and institutions of the new country too great a burden. Moreover, up to the World War nobody in this country cared whether immigrants learned, and even whether they became citizens or not. It was only in the cities and where their votes were needed that the immigrants were urged—and generally helped—to become citizens.

The same causes which have always delayed naturalization—except the desire to go back home—exist today and call for intelligent attention. With such attention there are reasons for the conviction that the whole problem may within reasonable time be largely liquidated. First, there should be increased facilities for aliens to learn the language of the country by providing more evening courses for adults, and more attention to the children of the newcomers in our public schools. It would be desirable that these children receive some special attention from the teachers so that they might learn not only a better use of the language, but all the best the teachers could give them about this country and its institutions and the American people. Every such child would soon become an effective agent of Americanization in its own home and its circle of acquaintances. Civilized countries today are giving more and more care to their backward children—how much more worthwhile would be a little special care given the child of the foreign-born in this country. Even such differences as foreign accents and strange un-American names which retard the understanding between the old and the new American, and hinder full national unity.

And then I would bespeak a greater facility for acquiring citizenship to the old people, who have been here for many years, worked in America, and have American born children and even grandchildren, but have never learned enough English to pass the usual present-day examination.

Those are my main suggestions for the speedier Americanization of the stranger within our gates!

ALES HRDLICKA was born in Humpoleo, Bohemia, of an old Czech family and in 1882, seeking better economic conditions, he came to the United States with his parents. He entered night school in New York and helped support his family with a daytime job. Soon after passing his medical exams in 1889 he became a research interne at Middletown (N. Y.) State Hospital. Later he took post-graduate studies at the University of Paris and at the Paris Anthropological School. From 1899 to 1903 Dr. Hrdlička was in charge of medical and anthropological researches on the Indians of the Southwest and Mexico under the auspices of the American Museum of Natural History. Since 1903 he has been associated with the Smithsonian Institute as Director of the Division of Physical Anthropology. Spry and hardy at 72, Dr. Hrdlička is still one of America's most active scientists.

by Dr. Otto Struve

THOSE OF US who are proud of our newly acquired American citizenship have had much food for thought during this past year while war has been raging on the other side of the Atlantic in native countries. I hope many foreign-born Americans read this for I want to send my greeting to all of them, especially those who, like myself, came to America to escape from the intolerable oppression of the dictators. I want to ask them to remember what they have left, and to consider with me what life would be to us now if we had not come to this free and peaceful land.

Since war broke out in Europe last year I have many times in my mind relived the days when as a refugee from war-torn Russia, I worked chopping wood in the Sultan's own forests near Constantinople, or when I carried bricks for a Turkish contractor in the Pera, or when

I did carpenter work in an American college on the shores of the Bosporus. And then an offer came for me to go to America! I remember gratefully the genial secretary of the American YMCA—every Russian pronounced it "Imca"—who helped me with the visas in Constantinople, and those other friendly Americans who had confidence in a young and untried student from Russia and made it possible for him to come to their country.

I arrived in New York nineteen years ago on a boat whose name particularly impressed me,—it was called the *Hog Island* of the United States Shipping Board. As we came up the harbor, New York looked strange, a little forbidding, a little too vast and too impersonal, and yet I was drawn to it by an irresistible force. I thought, "Here is opportunity! Here is freedom! Here perhaps I shall find success!"

Some people say that opportunity has vanished in this country. I know from my own experience that this is not true; America still offers opportunities that hard work will bring within our grasp. There isn't another country in the world today where there is as much tolerance toward persons of foreign birth and where merit is the only standard by which a man is measured. Only in America, I am convinced, would I have been permitted to follow my own inclinations and become a scientist, and only in America could I have found the opportunities to pursue my chosen occupation of an astronomer.

Astronomers try to find out more about the universe, to unravel the secret laws of nature, to discover the mysterious process by means of which ordinary substances —hydrogen, iron, calcium—are made to release power in the stars at the rate of hundreds of thousands of horse power over periods of time measured in millions or even billions of years. The quest for new knowledge always demands opportunity. At night I observe the stars through the largest refracting telescope in existence, located at the Yerkes Observatory of the University of Chicago at Williams Bay, Wisconsin. Every time I use this great telescope, I think with admiration of those resourceful and public-spirited Americans who fifty years ago had the vision to create a tool of scientific research more powerful than anything then in existence. And don't let anyone say that this type of opportunity is a thing of the past. The 82-inch telescope recently erected on a mountain in Texas stands as a memorial to the spirit of a rugged pioneer who made a fortune through hard work and who was inspired by the spirit of America to devote this fortune to the advancement of knowledge.

We astronomers today are the most fortunate men on this distressed globe. Through our telescopes we are able to escape to happier worlds where there are no such things as men and man-made troubles. Sometimes when I see through my telescope, millions of light years away, countless galactic universes each consisting of millions of blazing suns, a feeling of our own insignificance creeps

116

over me. What are we on our little planet, atoms of creation!

While men are dwarfed by the study of astronomy, this science more than any other makes one realize that knowledge is the most important thing humanity possesses. Knowledge has made us what we are. It was knowledge that guided Benjamin Franklin's hand when he set up the first lightning rod in Philadelphia; it was also knowledge which in the brain of the great English astronomer, Sir Norman Lockyer, led to the discovery of the gas helium in the sun. It was knowledge which brought about the invention of aeroplanes by the American astronomer Langley, and the American engineers, the Wright brothers. But it is also knowledge, misapplied knowledge, which in the hands of a dictator, has led to the most ghastly event of all history, the attacks on London.

It seems clear that knowledge can develop only in a free country where men can think without governmental supervision and where the search for truth and truth alone is permitted and encouraged. I have lived under the czars in Russia and under the commissars when the old regime collapsed. I know what it means to a scientist, a searcher after truth, to have to work for a government which uses every imaginable means of coercion to make its scholars say that black is white. Has not the science of astronomy been degraded in Russia to become a weapon for anti-religious propaganda? Has not the science of anthropology been compelled in Germany to promote the ludicrous theories of Aryan superiority? It may be that America will soon become the trustee of Truth for the whole world! That would be a great responsibility, but without some such guardianship mankind may very possibly find itself back among the superstitions of the Dark Ages.

As an astronomer, I must mention the spread of astrology in some of the totalitarian countries. Astrology is particularly dangerous because it is a perversion of science usually presented with the trimming and nomenclature of true science. In a country where independent thinking may be considered a crime, erroneous ideas can easily gain a firm hold. I am not surprised, therefore, when I read in the newspapers reports passed by European censorship that the head of one of the fascistic countries is a firm believer in the prognostications of the astrologers. Let me assure you here and now that the claims of astrology are false, that there is no foundation for the belief that the position of a planet among the fixed stars can appreciably influence our lives, the weather, the harvest or the outcome of a military campaign in Europe.

I regret that astrology is by no means dead in this country and I believe that it is intrinsically as pernicious to human progress as the cult of the so-called "superior races." It is based upon prejudice and emotion and not upon experiment and clear thinking. We must defend ourselves from subversive attempts to substitute emotion for logic. The greatest danger this country has experienced in its entire history is not the threat of an attack by a hostile fleet on our shores, or an invasion of parachute troops. It is the infiltration of fallacious ideas of the pseudo-scholars of the totalitarian countries. I wish I could shout to every man and woman in America, "Beware of the fifth column in the world of ideas! Don't let the emotional character of some of these false theories of science, economics, and government mislead you and divert you from the course of progress. Remember that the best thinkers in totalitarian Europe are prevented by force and duress from making the results of their findings known to you."

Ideas may be as dangerous to Democracy as dynamite. We have only to look abroad at other countries to see that they make a greater breach in a nation's defenses than cannons or bombers. In the same way our thinkers, scientists and teachers are the best defenders of democratic ideals and institutions. That is why they are the first victims of those who would overthrow Democracy. I could write about the banishment of eminent scientists, the purges, executions and traceless disappearances of some of the world's greatest astronomers, physicists, and chemists in some European countries. These facts are well known. The point I wish to make is that knowledge, science, culture itself are in actual danger of disappearing from the world. America and the few remaining

Democracies are the only places where civilization, accumulated painfully over thousands of years, can and must be saved from the modern barbarians who threaten its existence.

We are not alone in this faith. In the totalitarian countries of Europe are countless numbers of people who long for the freedom we enjoy here. The Pilgrims came from Europe to America because they preferred the wilderness to the religious oppression of Europe, and later other immigrants followed them seeking the same freedom from oppression. Today, for millions of homeless, harassed, and heartsick people the only hope is now that the torch of our freedom will shine so bright that it will sooner or later dispel the fog of bewilderment and oppression which has darkened their lives.

I was an officer in the old Russian army and was wounded in the struggle for liberty and decency in the old world. In America I have found that liberty which I longed for. I know that I express the feelings of most naturalized American citizens when I say that we shall without hesitation always defend our American liberty and our civilization.

OTTO STRUVE was born in Southern Russia and, like his father, grandfather and great grandfather, studied and became an astronomer. He served in the Russian army during the World War and later as a junior officer in the Caucasian Army against the Turks. In 1920 he escaped the Red Terror and became a laborer in Con-

120

stantinople. In the meantime he received an offer from Professor Edwin B. Frost of the Yerkes Observatory to come to America as his assistant. To Dr. Frost, whose successor Struve became in 1932, he owes his opportunity for continuing his astronomical work. To his wife, a native of Michigan, he owes his Americanization.

by Claudette Colbert

I THINK I WAS AT HOME in America *chez moi,* as the French say, from the very first. Politically, my father fell in love with America at once. He took out his papers immediately and nothing could have induced him to go back. But when a little French family transfers itself to some spot of the globe outside of France, it keeps a great many of its French qualities and its French customs.

In our little apartment, certainly, we were very foreign. Black butter on our shirred eggs,—croissants and chocolate for breakfast, lilies of the valley on the first of May to bring luck; avoid currents of air if you had a cold. And for years and years I was under the impression that if you took a bath before two hours after eating you died instantly, practically as you struck the water!

And then, of course, there were the proprieties—the things it was "comme il faut" for a little girl to say and do and think. There is something very lovely in that reverence with which transplanted French people cherish their culture and their customs. I think it was Alexander Woollcott who said they were like people curving their fingers around the flame of a candle to keep it burning on a windy night.

That love of country has kept the French from emigrating as much as most peoples. Comparatively few among America's foreign-born citizens or alien visitors are French. A Frenchman was once asked about this and his reply was revealing. "Why should we French travel when we are already there?"

I am sure my parents were homesick for a while in spite of their happiness in their new country. But I was a child growing up in this new windy civilization, going to school, making friends, learning American slang—and loving it all! Mighty questions would be raised at home as to whether it was proper for me, and the other girls I'd come to know at school to go to the movies all by ourselves. "Non! . . . *Non!* . . . NON!" For a well brought up French girl "Ce n'est pas possible!"

"But I'm not a French girl!" I'd insist, "I'm an American!" America represented everything that was free and fun and sensible, and the rightful inheritance of my generation. It was a land meant for young people, something to make you love a country wildly, not very intelligently perhaps, but with all your heart!

You feel that sense of hope in the air of America. I

loved that France from which I was once removed. I was proud of her as a legend—as though I had a very rich and elegant grandmother and France was her stately home. I got to know it first-hand when I made my first success in the theatre and went abroad. I found it incomparably beautiful—but, to revert to the simile of my grandmother's house, you like to go to it, and wander through the big rooms and think of the life that once was lived there, and then suddenly you want to get away! It represents a remote life—you want your own life, immediate and absorbing. I think it was in France that I began really to appreciate America in an adult way. Its possibilities for living, its simplicity and generosity and friendliness, its lovely lack of high walls, its easy attitude toward money. And then, its youth . . . life before it instead of behind! Suddenly I knew what a privilege it was to be an American. I wish devoutly I could do more to deserve that privilege!

That's why I don't hate the fifteenth of March as every right-minded tax-payer is supposed to! Except for taxes, being an American has been nothing but gravy for me. Certainly, after what America has done for me nobody but an ungrateful idiot could begrudge them.

Then, France fell! . . . I said I had felt toward France as though it were a grandmother's house, *my grandmother!* And then, suddenly, that lovely old house was in the hands of vandals. It saddened me infinitely and frightened me too. My grandmother's house was gone! What of my house . . . *our* house? What if the fire spread and the flood rose?

One thing that helped me through those terrible months was that I was working on a picture into which was woven the story of the fall of France. In it I played an American war correspondent who has been with the German army while her fiancé has been a volunteer in the Royal Air Force. The last scene of the picture is in the Forest of Compiègne where the Armistice is being signed. There I meet the flier whose arm has been broken. He says bitterly that he has to crawl back to America on some refugee ship and find some cushy job teaching kids to fly . . . That's a fine end! I'm grateful for what I had to say to him . . .

"The end? You don't think this is the end! Just because in that railway coach this afternoon they'll be clicking their heels and saying that freedom is a sign of weakness and incompetence; and that slavery is a badge of pride and patriotism! Oh, no! No, that can't be the end! You're not crawling back—we're marching back, both of us! . . . Tom, I've been watching them now for ten months, there are things I've got to say! My voice isn't much, I know, but I want to use it without somebody's hand over my mouth! And you—Oh, what a job you've got! . . . Making tens of thousands of pilots for tens of thousands of planes! . . . Remember your prayer? This time we have to say it

to America. 'Arise, my love. Arise! Be strong so you can
stand up straight and say to anyone under God's heaven:
All right, whose way of life shall it be—yours or ours?' "

CLAUDETTE COLBERT was born in Paris and came
to the United States in 1910 as a small girl. She attended
Washington Irving High School in New York City and
made her stage debut in 1924, later appearing in many
stage successes. She began her motion picture career in
1929 and achieved immediate acclaim for her fine per-
formances, among them in "It Happened One Night"
for which she received the Academy Award for the best
acting in 1934.

by Emil Ludwig

I HAVE BEEN TO AMERICA many times since I first began my wanderings in search of a homeland. I suppose I am the oldest German emigrant among the artists for I left my native land in 1906. Thirty-five years ago! But why did you leave there? What were you seeking that you didn't find at home?

I was always in love with Liberty. I did not care for the "Unteroffizier" at Breslau, where I was born. I did not like to be shouted at by the clerk in the post-office, because as a boy when buying stamps I dared to tap at his window when I saw he was eating his sandwiches during office hours and letting a row of people wait at his counter. I was already too democratic in my views to believe that every man in a uniform—and you know that every State or private official in Germany wears a uniform—is superior to a civilian.

When I left home I went to the oldest republic—
Switzerland, the only country that can be compared to
the United States for liberty of everyday life as well as
government.

I believe Switzerland to be the model for the United
States of Europe which will come in one way or the
other after this war. Switzerland has proved by its history of centuries that you can have a national unity with
three different languages and three so-called "races."
What federation does here for 130 millions of men, the
Swiss do over there for 4 millions. They also have self-
governing States only much smaller ones, called Cantons
. . . 22 of them. It is the only democracy with a refer-
endum—the submission of proposed laws to the vote of
the people for rejection or acceptance. And in some
Cantons they still have the old custom of an open-air
gathering of the people, where they elect their leading
governors by acclamation. Switzerland is also the only
place where the government so entirely trusts its citizens
that every soldier in service takes his gun home to his
house with 80 cartridges, and the cavalry even keep their
horses at home when not in service. They believe that
national defense like patriotism begins at home and
every man protects his land and house. Their history
and geography show that they are no country of conquest for the Swiss are the only Europeans that never
had a king.

Why then did I leave? you ask. That is easy to answer.

The Swiss are absolutely surrounded by totalitarian States. The country is a trap. The Nazis don't like me very much—my writings did them great harm. So I didn't care to provoke difficulties for the Swiss Government which is duty bound to remain neutral and to avoid provocations.

The fact that I am here today in America is one good testimony to its advantages and virtues. If I were a man escaping the Nazi hell you would expect me to be enthusiastic. But for someone coming from the very sister-land of liberty to admire America as I do is real praise.

I did go back to Germany from time to time after my emigration to Switzerland, every year for a few weeks and during all of the World War. Since 1932 I have not returned there. But I was a Swiss citizen for a longer time than Mr. Hitler has been a German citizen anyway.

It has become a little commonplace to repeat for the hundredth time the comparison between the American paradise of Liberty and the hell of totalitarianism. But when I see life here and look back to what I saw even in European democracies like England and France before this war—and I was in France to the end of May, 1940— I should like to remind every American I meet of the advantages he has in this great country. Comparisons can never be exact, but I would like to make some today, nevertheless between the American customs and those of several other countries. These by-ways, these "nuances" are more interesting to me than the principles of government which you are reading no end in your papers and magazines nowadays.

There is so little color in this much-abused word "Democracy," so little to feel and to smell about it. I prefer the word *liberty* about which Goethe once said: "This word is so beautiful, that we must love it—even if it should turn out to be an error."

Let me tell you some small items of everyday life that I have noticed everywhere in this country; east and west. Firstly, the open face and smile that people are wont to show one another here. It is natural to Americans to trust; and natural to Europeans to distrust one another. There is struggle here as everywhere:—but co-operation seems more natural to you than seclusion. There is less privacy here but more comradeship than in Europe. The gardens around your pretty cottages and bungalows have no fences, their lawns open out quickly to the street, no hedge separates them from the neighboring garden. That fact impressed me on my first visit, and I suppose most of all because I had just come from where they are so exclusive that they do not even put their names on the entrance door of their apartments.

I have found any amount of other virtues in our everyday life. For instance, the question "Can I help you?" I have found it nowhere else, and it comes naturally to everybody here. If I have lost my way with my car and drop into a filling station to ask for a street, here the young man smilingly looks it up for me in his book, shows it to me on the map with complete civility, even presents his map to me without expecting me to buy fuel or to tip him. I know, of course, that this friendliness is good business—but in Europe you can go far to find this smile and courteousness which is bestowed on me even though I am not a pretty girl— In the same situation the Frenchmen looks up from his garage work and asks rather sullenly, "Qu'est-ce que vous desirez, Monsieur?" or the Italian, "?Rome, Cosa cerca Signori"—meaning the same; whereas in Berlin the tone would be even menacing: "Sie Wünchen?" Can I help you?—a truly American form of civil life, symbolizing co-operation and trustfulness!

Here's another example of your general companionship. The offices of your banks, factories, editorials, newspapers are generally in one big hall with hardly any partitions to separate one desk from the other. All work together, all can see one another, and even the manager or editor is only divided from the rest by a glass partition wall. But I was more astonished yet when I noticed that in some of your older government buildings in Washington the doors to the offices did not reach the floor.

I then thought of the heavy carpeted floors and forbidding doors of London's Downing Street 10, or the French Foreign Office on the Quai d'Orsay, where a liveried footman carefully opens and closes the double doors after having announced your arrival to the Minister as he would announce a King. . . . Even in the White House, when in the waiting-room, I heard the President's secretary dictating a letter while close to him other visitors were talking and laughing. . . . All this informality and open-mindedness impressed every European, not just the trembling man from a totalitarian State!

European ministries and State offices are completely different. They are ceremonial. The Quai d'Orsay at Paris still continues the style of courts 70 years after the last emperor. It is an old Palace, purple silk, red tapestry, many solemn servants in the ante-chambers. . . . Electric lights are always turned on, because so little light enters through the heavy silken curtains . . . visitors sit along the walls on stiff chairs waiting their turn in solemn silence. Nobody would dare to speak to his neighbor. General distrust!

The absence of solemnity seems to me a great item in America. It is the only country I know that hangs a caricature of its President in the visitors' waiting-room of the Executive Mansion!

I have had the honor of being received by the last three Presidents. I remember once I saw at the White House a symbolical act of your democratic manners. A young visitor was talking to the President at his desk and receiving from him a cigarette, he lighted it by striking the match on the sole of his shoe—all this in the immediate presence of the first man of the country—

who did not even notice it. I can never forget this young American Prometheus.

On the 4th of July while I was working on his biography, I was invited by President Roosevelt to his home in Hyde Park, New York. In London or Paris I saw on the National Festival nothing but parades, uniforms, speeches, and police, police, police! Do you know what I encountered in Hyde Park? A dozen young people in swimming suits, gathered around a pool, and in it—and under an old apple tree the President in shirt sleeves sitting as a Patriarch on the lawn, conversing with a State Secretary and some old friends who had turned up to celebrate the national holiday.

I think this all springs from America's preference to take life humorously. You dislike tragedy as you dislike pompousness. For two months I had the honor to serve as a professor at the State College of Santa Barbara. The other evening I took part at the annual faculty dinner; a collection of highly cultivated, serious men and women. I compared this assembly with similar evenings I had witnessed in Germany in my youth, when my father was a Professor, and later as a guest in Paris and Rome universities. It would be impossible for a big number of European professors to be entertained in so gay and humorous a way as I witnessed among my colleagues of Santa Barbara. Fun, irony, parody for everybody and not the least pretentiousness. All these American traits and characteristics would seem to provide an inner natural defense against dictatorship. And above all I think that America's fitness and willingness for humor is her great antidote against dictators. A dictator always is gloomy and sullen. You cannot be a laughing tyrant. The whole nation would laugh at a man giving himself airs —you do not accept sinister faces even among your headlines. Your curiosity about the private life of everybody, your newspaper headings about divorces and marriages come from your cheerful acceptance of life.

Is America as a nation sympathetic and understanding toward those who come to us from other lands? That is a question that has great importance for us refugees. I think from what I have seen that you warmly welcome the foreigner. You have the will to give him a chance amongst you—you like to learn from him and to let him partake of your inheritance. I believe that this spirit is known to the world and that is why the homeless and disinherited of the earth look to America as the land of hope today even as the Pilgrims looked at it—the land where men are still friendly and free! In return emigrants love you for this—even those who have great difficulties in making their way here.

EMIL LUDWIG was born in Germany in 1881 and educated at Breslau and Heidelberg. He began his literary career as a dramatist and wrote plays exclusively for almost twelve years. Only after his thirtieth birthday did he write prose. At an early date he left Germany, making

134

his home in Switzerland and traveling extensively gathering material for his many books, most of them biographies, "Napoleon", "Bismarck", "Goethe", etc. Several years ago he came to the United States to make his permanent home here.

by Dr. Stephen S. Wise

FOUR HUNDRED AND FIFTY YEARS ago the ships of Columbus sailed to discover this continent. On the same day they sailed, Jewish dwellers in Spain were driven forth from their long-time homes into exile in strange lands. No one connected those two events, nor guessed that America was to become the hope of all freedom-loving people, dispossessed of their heritage in their own lands. Today, unhappy millions turn their eyes to America, asking whether it will still offer refuge to Liberty and Justice. History is waiting breathlessly for the answer to the question—what is a real American today?

Americanism must be something more than a geographical designation if it is to meet its present responsibilities of preserving human dignity and freedom for posterity. One is not necessarily an American because one was born here. I remember a conversation I had once with Theodore Roosevelt. He had asked me whether my father had been born in America. "No, Colonel," I told him, "my dear father was born in Eger, Hungary, and did not come here until he was a man." "That is strange," said he, "he always seemed to me a native American."

"On the day after Lincoln's death," I told Colonel Roosevelt, "he and some friends at a German University were discussing America. One of them sighed and said, 'some day I would like to go to that land of gold!' 'I,' said another, 'would like to go to the land of steel.' 'And I,' said a third, 'would like to go to the land of cotton.'

"My father spoke up then. 'I want to live in the land of Lincoln!' " Ten years later he came to America.

Teddy Roosevelt brought his hand down in that familiar gesture. "Bully!" he cried. "I should say, Dr. Wise, that your father was a good American ten years before he came to this country!"

And he was right! America was settled by Americans from all lands! People who shared the same ideals of life. They were spiritually akin. They had a common faith, a common way of thinking, which is the secret of American unity. We are here a nation of people drawn from all parts of the globe, but one in our determination to become free and equal. We have brought the ideas of freedom and just human relationships here with us on ships since the beginning. We did not find the conception of Democracy waiting ready-made in the forests of the New World. I am proud to believe that the mosaic theocracy—which means Democracy under God—of the Jewish immigrants—has contributed to the American ideal. On the outer rim of the bell in Independence Hall, which on the fourth of July, 1776 burst forth with the most joyous tidings that ever greeted the ears of listening men, is inscribed the command taken from the testament of the Hebrew Bible—"And ye shall proclaim Liberty throughout the land unto all the inhabitants thereof."

We have drawn upon the best thinking of all nations —the English colonists brought the Magna Carta and the Bill of Rights with them as their heritage. And think how much Jefferson and Franklin and the other writers of the Declaration of Independence and the Constitution learned from the writings of Rousseau and the other great French philosophers! The Scandinavians too have brought splendid contributions to the formulation of the American creed from a thousand years of thinking in terms of human relationships. Yes, Americans have come from all lands where standards are based not on money, but manhood, not descent but ascent, not acquisition but aspiration, not color but character. There is an inscription on a monument to the American pioneers which gives an answer to the question, 'What is a real American?' It reads, "The cowards never started, the weak died on the way." It is not a light or easy thing to leave one's native background for the hope of a better way of life. That is why I have faith in the ability of Americanism to stand the test of today.

Our newer Americans, being closer to the pioneer urge which drove men to seek freedom and opportunity in this country should be among the strongest defenders of America. And I believe that the overwhelming majority of them are fervid patriots. Democracy is precious to them because it is an achievement and not an inheritance. The consciousness of being an American is always with me, while native-born Americans may forget their birthright because they take it so much for granted. Democracy is a faith and not a political or economic system. I am of the opinion that all Americans had better again renew some of the emotional spirit that led our forefathers across oceans and through the wilderness to establish a land of liberty. In the words of the poet, "to rebuke the age's popular crime, we need the souls of fire, the hearts of that old time."

The experiment of popular government is far from being triumphantly concluded. We are pioneers still. Instead of being an old outworn form of government as its enemies claim, Democracy is the newest system of human relationships, still struggling to establish its ideas of equality, of opportunity, justice and human dignity in a world of ancient hates. What is there modern and new in the totalitarian conception of Force and Brute

Power ruling the lives of men? The people of my own race could testify that what is going on today is as old as history.

I was only one year old when my parents arrived in New York with their five children and established themselves in that city. Therefore, my life to all intents and purposes was that of a native-born American reared and educated in one of our great cities. I was well launched in my career before I realized that all that I knew of America was New York City, or of Americans were the then four million inhabitants of New York. I felt that that was not enough—I wanted to bathe in the waters of unpolluted Americanism, and so I deliberately accepted a call to a synagogue in Oregon, as far away from the familar scenes of my youth as possible. The result of this experiment in Americanization was astonishing! A new America was opened to me—an America I should never have known if I had remained in one part of the country. I believe that no one can be spiritually a real American unless he knows the different people, their lives and souls and their viewpoints of this great country and realizes with pride what wonders are comprised in that word—"American."

National defense needs not only guns and airplane bases to protect our nation from aggressors. Our greatest defense of Democracy is the burning faith deep in the hearts of every American that what we have here, or what we can have, is worth every sacrifice that may be necessary. It is this conviction alone that will protect us from confusion, disillusion and hopelessness which has created totalitarian dictatorships.

I would not be here—nor eight million other foreign-born American citizens—today without that faith. In the midst of the turmoil of an unhappy world, faith that here in America is still justice, opportunity and liberty is bringing on every ship and clipper plane the artists, writers, and thinkers of every land who can work and live only where they are free. This world crisis may be America's opportunity to become the greatest civilization the world has ever known. Here, in the words of Emerson, is what the earth waits for. We speak of history as though it were only the Past, but we ourselves are history. What will be said of you and me by those who live in this nation a hundred years hence? Let us make it possible for those who are to come after us to say, "They kept the promises America made in the beginning. Democracy was entrusted to them and they defended it not only from foes without, but within; from intolerance, inertia, ignorance, and private ambition. Liberty was entrusted to them and they preserved it for the future."

I have already hinted at some of the things which our American Democracy borrowed from or was influenced by in the shaping of the spiritual and political fortunes of the Republic. It was not fortuitous that on Independence Bell were and still are engraved the words of the Hebrew Bible:

141

"Ye Shall Proclaim Liberty Throughout the Land
Unto All the Inhabitants Thereof."

It was not fortuitous that in an early Constitution of the
Massachusetts Colony, it is stated that any questions that
arise, the answers to which are not here given, shall be
referred for solution to the Hebrew Pentateuch, which is
the Constitution of the Mosaic theocracy.

Nor least of all is it fortuitous that when something
more than fifty years ago, the French nation presented
to our country the figure of the statue which stands
and shines on Bedloe Island, in our Harbor, that there
should have been written on its base, some lines from
the pen of Emma Lazarus, gifted American poetess,
friend of Emerson, cousin to the late Justice of the Supreme Court, Benjamin Nathan Cardozo. And these
were the words:

Not like the brazen giant of Greek fame,
With conquering limbs astride from land to land,
Here at our sea-washed sunset gates shall stand
A mighty woman with a torch, whose flame
Is the imprisoned lightning, and her name
Mother of Exiles. From her beacon-hand
Glows world-wide welcome; her mild eyes command
The air-bridge harbour that twin cities frame.
"Keep, ancient lands, your storied pomp!" cried she
With silent lips. "Give me your tired, your poor,

Your huddled masses yearning to breathe free.
The wretched refuse of your teeming shore.
Send these, the homeless, the tempest-tossed to me.
I lift my lamp beside the golden door!"

To which I would only add, it is not only "The new Colossus" that cries:

"I lift my lamp beside the golden door!"

It is the liberty-loving stranger, who comes to the shore and door of our country, who takes the beloved lamp and is prepared to carry it on, to hold it aloft for the enlightenment and benediction of America and to serve as healing and blessing to unnumbered generations of those who cherishing freedom more than life, would fain become citizens of our immortal Republic.

STEPHEN S. WISE was born in Budapest in 1872 and was brought to the United States soon after. He received his degree from Columbia University in 1892 and immediately became pastor of the Congregation of the Madison Avenue Synagogue, New York (1893–1900) and of Beth Israel, Portland, Oregon. In 1907 he founded the Free Synagogue of New York of which he was thenceforth rabbi. Besides gaining a great reputation as an eloquent preacher, Dr. Wise became widely known as a publicist, Zionist and as a leader in social welfare work.

by Giuseppe Bellanca

SOME AMERICANS SEEM TO FEEL that we newcomers ought to forget as quickly as possible the memories, traditions and customs we bring to this country from every part of the World. It is a great pity to confuse a man's political loyalties with his taste for his native cookery and preference for the wines of his fatherland; as if patriotism had anything to do with the palate. And it certainly doesn't mean that a naturalized American of Italian birth is a fascist because he loves the literature and scenery of Italy!

It would be short-sighted to condemn a man for his culture if his political connections are American. This country needs and uses the cultural characteristics of all of the newcomers. In fact, with the rich gifts they bring we could build up here on this continent a civilization greater than any the World has ever known. I believe that this will happen now that great artists, scientists, writers and thinkers are coming to the United States to find the freedom which is denied them today in so many lands.

Democracy will work in America! Here it is different, our leaders and representatives are elected for a reasonable period of service and have time to work out their plans like men running a business. In many of the democracies which have fallen the entire personnel of government was changed sometimes once a month. New officials with new ideas and plans had no opportunity to put them to the test before they also were out of power! As a businessman, I know you couldn't run an industrial plant that way—changing its methods with every whiff of opposition.

I believe that American businessmen will not let Democracy fail in this country because they are beginning to realize that private initiative cannot exist under any other government. I believe all Americans—rich, poor, even jobless Americans, prefer to live under a system that offers the possibility of advancement and reward for effort and a gambler's chance for success. As soon as our businessmen see clearly that self-interest as well as patriotism demand the defense of Democracy they will turn to the task of making it work just as they buckle down to solving a tough problem in their own business.

The defense of Democracy is a business as well as a

military problem. It must give people work and security as well as battleships and bombers! The question is, how? Private business may depend on the preservation of popular government, but will it realize its danger and responsibility in time?

I am an American businessman, and I know many others. I know that by and large, they are reasonable, enterprising, adaptable and patriotic. I believe that they are men of good-will. But human nature is not perfect, and they are also, in some cases, self-centered. They have had to be in order to build and develop their own businesses. Some of them have perhaps kept their eyes fixed on their own ledgers, machines and products without glancing often enough through their factory windows at the rest of the World. They have grown to regard the rules of business as having no connection with society.

And now, suddenly, they are expected to enlarge their business rules to include the needs of people in general —people they have thought of as customers, buyers of their product, and not in any other way connected with them. Suddenly they are asked to adapt private capitalism to the public good. Our Big Business has been the pride of a young and ambitious country—its heads have been looked up to, admired—now suddenly they feel that they are being blamed for conditions they have never thought were their responsibility. They are good Americans—they would fight if need be to defend America, and they are astonished and hurt to find that some people blame them for the troubles of the World. They may have been short-sighted, but they have run business as they always ran it and people come to think that because a thing is usual, it is also right.

Business has adapted itself to technological change—why not social change? I think the present emergency with trade overturned in many countries may shock Americans into the realization that we must adjust ourselves to new needs and conditions if we wish to keep our way of life. The threat of the loss of private enterprise abroad will teach us that small changes are better than total loss, and nothing is more certain than that we must relinquish something in order not to lose everything. I talk to many businessmen and I know we are beginning to look out of our factory windows and think about our fellow Americans and their necessities as part of our business.

Perhaps we shall be led to share our opportunities and jobs and business profits and American standards of living with each other from self-preservation at first. The War in Europe has shown us the preciousness of what we have over here and the necessity of holding on to it even at the cost of personal sacrifice. Danger may teach us what economists, reformers, and sociologists haven't. But after that, new viewpoints, new ways of thinking will have to come more slowly in the only way public change ever comes—through education of the people.

All Americans—native as well as foreign-born, need

to be educated to the modern meaning and practical problems of Democracy in an industrialized World and in competition with totally different ideologies. We're celebrating an anniversary of the Wright brothers' flying machine this year. It was the wonder of the World when it was built, but it wouldn't be adequate today. In the same way we must modernize and streamline our ideas of freedom to fit an industrial economy if we are to have in the America of today the same liberty and justice and opportunity the founders of this country intended. That means education—re-examination of Democracy in the light of new times.

Equality of opportunity is only a phrase to a man on relief. The American people must have a stake in Democracy to defend it. The President, the Congress, cannot give them this stake. Only industry can do that. Therefore, I say, let us educate our businessmen in the aims of Democracy as well as our naturalized aliens and our school children. It is the best way of life for human beings. I am sure of it—a man wants to do something by himself, of himself, for himself! That is why Americans are so enterprising, so inventive, so much happier as a people than other peoples. They respect themselves instead of worshiping some leader.

It took free enterprise and the profit system to develop the airplane, for instance. And now man's cleverness and ingenuity is being used to destroy him! I love airplanes, they have been my whole life, but I am shocked at the power we have turned loose. Never before has there been such frightfulness in warfare—death rained from the skies on homes and villages and women and babies. My son saw it coming years ago. He came to me and said—"Dad, let's begin to dig!" But I did not believe it possible for the dream men have dreamed for centuries—that of flying above the earth—to become a nightmare—and yet perhaps there is a hope for mankind in this terrible total warfare.

GIUSEPPE BELLANCA was born in Sciacca, Italy in 1886 and received an education in mathematics and engineering at the Institute Tecnico, in Milan. He came to the United States in 1911 and established a laboratory for special research in aviation. Later he founded the Bellanca Aviation School. The first cabin monoplane in the U.S. was designed by Bellanca and he also built the first monoplanes to fly the Atlantic and the Pacific. Now head of the Bellanca Aircraft Corporation of America, Bellanca lives at Rockland, Delaware.

by Dr. Walter Damrosch

I REMEMBER MY ARRIVAL in America well. I was a boy, nine years old, when we arrived in New York with our father and mother. That was in 1871 and Germany was then experiencing just such an upheaval as we know today—only then men who loved the peace of the world and freedom and liberty of thought, suffered from the oppression of Prussian kings instead of a dictator. Many left their homes in Germany then, just as they are forced to do today and came to America where they could breathe and think freely and say what was in their minds —and were not afraid of persecution. And out of those troubled times abroad, America has gained some of her greatest patriots. For example Carl Schurz, who stood at Lincoln's side during the distress of our Civil War, and was responsible for many of our liberal political reforms as well as making other contributions to his adopted country.

My father was one of those who loved freedom and found it in America. He taught my brother, Frank, and myself our first lessons in Democracy along with our early training as musicians.

Music is the one great international language, and if through music we can create a feeling of universal brotherhood, isn't this just another way to express the ideals of Democracy? And that's what being an American means. Here we do not stop to ask a man what his racial antecedents may be—German, French, Italian, Norwegian, English—he is still an American. And so, if a man has a soul for music and learns to love it culturally, his nationality will not matter.

America is a composite of nations and peoples from all over the world who have come to us bringing their racial customs and music—a wealth of beauty. Through the intermingling of their arts they have created a national unity—and music as an international language is an important factor in our civilization. I remember Christmas in Germany, snow and jingle bells and sleighs! It is a holiday that is well loved there. Germany was first to have Christmas trees, and the legend of Santa Claus. . . . That good old St. Nicholas that all children love so dearly! But here in our own country we celebrate with *all* of these customs, and sing the carols of all lands. . . . Why, it doesn't matter whether it is "God Rest Ye Merry Gentlemen", which came to us from England, or "Noel, Noel" from France, or "When Christmas Morn is Breaking" from Norway, or "Come Little Children" from Denmark, or "Lullaby of Mary and the Angels" (Sleep My Little One), from Holland, or carols from *any* other country—you may hear them sung lustily in America.

I must admit the picture is dark today, but there is *even in Europe* one little country where you may find three races who have been living under one flag in peace and freedom together for more than six centuries. This tiny country has dwelt among quarrelsome neighbors without once being drawn into their turmoils since the Napoleonic era when it was invaded by other nations. It is Switzerland, of course. Switzerland is a symbol that should become the hope of Europe. A tiny country whose borders contain only 16,000 square miles; but she has twenty-five small States, or Cantons, as they are called there, whose varied races and languages make it necessary to publish all official Government proclamations in German, French and Italian. But under a truly democratic government they live in absolute peace with each other.

Centuries ago, music, like art, and the ability to read and write, and other cultural arts belonged principally to the so-called upper classes, but as man's freedoms have grown these gifts have been given to the people. So, loving music as I do, I wanted to show my love and appreciation for all that America has done for me by sharing my music. And so, following in my father's footsteps, I did what I could to make music truly democratic in my adopted land.

I went all over our country with my New York Symphony Orchestra and Opera Company, giving concerts and operas, even in places that had never heard such music before, for I wanted to teach Americans the beauty of the Masters of all civilized countries.

My first opera was the "Scarlet Letter", and the story was adopted from Hawthorne's novel of that name. It was in 1895 I composed that. The first performance was in Boston. In 1937 the Metropolitan Opera Company produced my opera, "The Man Without A Country", for which the poet Arthur Guiterman had written the libretto. You no doubt recall this patriotic story of Edward Everett Hale. Lieutenant Philip Nolan is on trial for conspiracy with Aaron Burr and at the court martial he makes an oath that he hopes he may never see or hear the name of the United States again—and his punishment is that he shall live in perpetual exile on an American ship and never set foot on American shores. But, contrite, he breathes almost as a last prayer these words . . . "Perhaps there is no man living or dead who has ever loved his country so much as I but deserved less at her hands."

This opera was later produced on the air so that millions of Americans might hear it instead of the few thousands who may have been sitting in the Metropolitan Opera House. And when you speak of radio, there is the greatest invention for Democracy that man has been given since the art of printing brought the Bible into the hands of the people. What a great assistant it has been to me in teaching music to my millions of students all over America—most of whom I may never see or know personally. But I should not have had the pleasure of teaching them had it not been for radio!

Every one wants to know how I came to start my Music Appreciation Hour. That idea really dates back to 1897 when I first began a series of orchestral concerts for boys and girls in New York, at which I explained the music which I played for them with my orchestra. Appreciation of great art is largely a matter of habit, and habits, good or bad, are formed more easily when one is young.

I think it was back about 1926 when I suggested to the National Broadcasting Company the idea of a music school over the air. They accepted this suggestion eagerly and during these fourteen years have given me the most generous co-operation. The plan worked! We started with an audience of about a million and a half and today it is estimated at seven million in the United States, Canada and as far west as Hawaii.

First I decided I should talk to my "students" just as though they were really before me. I told them about each instrument in the orchestra, how it sounded and then I played it for them. Next I told them what place it occupied in the orchestra, and then, more lessons, until they knew just the meaning of a great symphonic orchestra . . . each a different instrument with different sounds, but playing in harmony with all the others to make beautiful music!

Let us hope that someday, instead of being the bearer of ill news with wars and strifes of nations . . . that someday, radio will carry words that mean peace, and goodwill and understanding to men of all races—to men all over the world. And why not? There are letters that come pouring into my office from millions of my radio pupils expressing their ardent love and appreciation of music we have learned together. And if, if we could teach the people, peoples of all lands, everywhere, that nations must and can work together like the instruments of a great symphonic orchestra, each doing his job in a world that was created for everybody, then we could say, "Peace on earth, good will to men."

WALTER DAMROSCH was born in Breslau, Germany in 1862. He studied music under his father's tutelage and came to the United States with him in 1871. He became conductor of the Newark Harmonic Society in 1881 and in 1885 succeeded his father as Musical Director of the Oratorio and Symphony Society of New York. During the World War he reorganized the U.S. Army bands at the request of General Pershing. In 1920 Dr. Damrosch accepted official invitations from France, Italy and Belgium to tour Europe with the Symphony

Society of New York. This was the first European tour of an American orchestra. He pioneered in radio with the first concert on the air and in 1927 became Musical Counsel for the National Broadcasting Company. He is probably best known for his Music Appreciation Hour for children.

★ 24 ★

by Dr. Gaetano Salvemini

ITALIANS ARE QUICK-MINDED in their actions, but taking out citizenship papers in another country—that is another thing. I wanted to know America and understand her better. That is why I only became a citizen in 1940 while I've been coming to America since 1927.

I first came on a lecture tour and for three months I rushed from New York to Portland, Maine; then to Cleveland, Ohio; to Boston, and so forth. I learned little of America except her telephone poles, which I saw from the train, and her lecture halls. When I returned to Europe I told my friends, "When I die, put on my grave the following inscription: 'He survived a lecture tour in the United States'."

On my next trip in 1929 I found the small villages in America where life is slow and quiet and peaceful like that of my old Southern Italy, and in addition there were

157

all the comforts of modern civilization. You know most foreigners who come to America look for something here akin to their native land. I never cared for New York—it is noisy, exhausting and terrifying—and too big! But in 1930 when I was invited to become a visiting professor at Harvard, my eyes were opened to new wonders of America, your wonderful libraries mostly.

In European libraries sometimes a person must wait hours and hours, even days, and sometimes he never gets the books he wants. Working at the Widener Library at Harvard was a new and happy experience for me. In this country, libraries are made for the public and not for librarians, they are one of the finest flowers of American civilization. That's why I say that at Harvard I really began to discover the true United States and to love her. Since then I have discovered more and more of her with the result that I have loved her more and more! But Harvard alone is not the United States. It is only one of our University centers set in beautiful New England, but we have many other wonderful spots in our immense country—and, of course, we have our dark spots too.

Who can discover the whole of America? Each of us discovers as much of America as he can. No doubt the America I know is centered about the teachers, the young students and the intellectual classes. I know that among these people in America is an abundance of kindness, hospitality and good will. But there are other things here that make me love America even more.

I love America because I can go from Cambridge to Los Angeles, and from Minneapolis to New Orleans without anyone's being entitled to question me as to why I am going there and not elsewhere—what I will do there, how long will I stay there and whom I shall see there? I love this country because here I can say what I like without being obliged to look over my shoulder to see whether or not I'm being watched by spies. I love this country because here I can print my thoughts without censorship and choose my daily paper from among all shades of opinion.

In Europe where one has to beware of spies all individuals are rendered suspicious of each other. The man you talk to in the park, the train or in a restaurant may cause you harm, so you must be careful what you say to him. In a country where one has to salute the party in power, no person who has to earn his livelihood is allowed to live freely even though silently in his own little corner. He must come to the front and declare before his fellows that he bows to the dictator and considers his rule the best possible in the world. You see, the man who has no political spine can adhere to this—and is ready to change his politics as soon as circumstances change. But men of that stripe are merely puppets to a form of government.

To a man of his own convictions—what an appalling situation! If a man has no children, if he can find employment in foreign countries, and if he escapes being shot by frontier guards he emigrates and begins life afresh. But few men are in so fortunate a position. The majority are tied to the land, to their professions and their homes. These are the unhappy ones.

Anxiously but silently their mothers and wives await their decisions. Shall a man betray his faith and give in as many of his friends have already done? Many think it is useless to persevere in a resistance which will be broken sooner or later. Thus they take the first step. They give the official salute and after that there is no turning back.

Yet not even American Democracy is the perfect dream our forefathers planned for us. All forms of government are imperfect because they are all created by human beings, whose nature is imperfect. But I believe firmly that when people attack the democratic institutions of this nation they are making the same mistake that I made in Italy before the Fascist regime. I criticized with the intention of improving Italian Democracy, but others used this freedom to destroy it. And the same democratic rights which protected me, protected the destroyer. I do not say that I was wrong. I do say that sometimes it is not enough to be right. Right must be guided by wisdom and prudence. You see, I am like the dog who has been scalded by hot water— Now, I stay clear even of cold water. Actually I experience physical pain when I hear talk against Democracy.

Ask the recent exiles and refugees who also love these

freedoms and have come here now because in their own countries these precious rights have been lost! They compare the hell of European totalitarianism with the paradise of American Democracy. That is why we who have come from Europe are not amazed when the Austrian refugee on landing in New York kissed the earth of this land of liberty. Liberty is like light—like air! While one enjoys it, one attaches little importance to it. Only when one has lost it does he realize how hateful life is without its freedoms. Since I am so whole-hearted a believer in Democracy, why was I so reluctant in becoming an American, you ask.

Loving a country is not enough to take the oath of allegiance to it. An oath should be taken seriously. Kings often take their pledges lightly, but I am not a king. I come from Southern Italian peasant stock and I could not make a half-hearted promise to give my adopted country my loyalty. I will tell you about the Americanization of Gaetano Salvemini. You know how we often carry on mental conversations with ourselves. One day I was enjoying America thus when suddenly I thought ... "What a great pity that I was not born in this country." Then later, another day, I was reading my daily newspaper when I found I was not so interested in news from Europe, but what President Roosevelt said in an address, and what Mr. Hoover said, and then a story about Mayor La Guardia, and I found myself taking sides in their controversies pro and con. ... Then I knew I was

161

becoming an American! The oath I pledged myself to read when I became a citizen: "I absolutely and entirely renounce and abjure all allegiance and fidelity to any foreign prince, potentate, state or sovereignty," was easy for I renounced my loyalties to the rulers of Italy when I left in 1925 because I was unable to live under a totalitarian form of government. But never did I renounce my love for the country of my birth and for the people in whose civilization I was brought up. Sometimes the foreign-born find that difficult to understand when they want to become Americans—thus, they are often divided in their loyalties. For myself, I settled this before asking for my papers.

The oath also states: "I will support and defend the Constitution and laws of the United States of America against all enemies, foreign and domestic." And to this I would repeat the reply that an American citizen of German extraction gave to the formula, "My country right or wrong." His answer was "to keep my country right, if it is right, to make it right if it is wrong."

Countless thousands of men are shedding their blood or living under the nightmare of war in Europe today as a result of the crazy policies of two criminal men and their accomplices—a war which the people have no heart for. I am sorry—deeply sorry for the people in the land of my birth—yet if the United States fought a war against totalitarian principles, I would bear arms, even against my native land but with a tragic feeling of unhappiness.

And once the war was won, I would urge America to dispense a just peace, not only to Italy, but to all countries for that is our only hope of a lasting peace.

GAETANO SALVEMINI was born in Molfetta, Italy, in 1873 and was educated at the University of Florence. From 1901 through 1908 he was Professor of History at the University of Messina and later occupied the same chair at the University of Pisa and the University of Florence. Dr. Salvemini was a member of the Italian Chamber from 1919–1921 and as early as June, 1925, was an avowed enemy of Fascism. In that month he was arrested for his anti-Fascist pronouncements and two months later resigned his position and left Italy. Since that time Dr. Salvemini has been a noted professor in American universities. In 1934 he became Lecturer on the History of Italian Civilization at Harvard University.

by Elissa Landi

IN AUGUST 1930 the *S.S. Aquitania* carried, as one of its first class passengers, a young actress on her way to New York and a role in a Broadway production that made her the envy of every other Broadway actress of her age. She had left Southampton with the blessing of an affectionate family and the good wishes of a host of friends, her stateroom filled with flowers, candy and books, and the assurance that she would be back soon. England had harbored her for the past seventeen years, although it had never been her country. It had entertained her hospitably. And now she was off to visit the United States, because that's one of the things one does when one has the chance, because it is civilized to have been to America and a good thing to have played on Broadway if one is an actor.

"Don't expect European manners," one friend had warned her. "No one in America has time for those little courtesies you're used to. The men will grab you by the arm crossing streets and think that's manners, but the next minute they'll push into a room ahead of you!"

"American girls are prettier than we are," said another, "but they lack charm, they lack femininity, they're too much in competition with men. And they're spoiled. They're hard."

"Taxi-drivers and servants aren't respectful the way they are over here. Lift boys tell you to 'step on it' and policemen shout at you."

The young actress was a little frightened but presumed that she would be able to stick it out for the run of the play anyway.

It struck her as strange that, on the boat, the politest passengers appeared to be those boorish Americans. They alone seemed interested in telling her what she should see when she arrived in New York, where she should stay and shop and eat. They also spoke to her as if they already knew her whereas the European passengers seemed to be waiting for an introduction—which was never forthcoming as she didn't know anyone on the boat.

I know all about her experiences. Of course. I was that actress.

We arrived on August 15th and docked with a minimum of fuss, which if you are used to docking at Marseilles or climbing into a tender out of a French boat at Southampton, is already a remarkable feat.

A gay Irish customs man joked with me as he inspected my luggage. (Oh, I thought Americans were too much in a hurry to take time off to make jokes.)

Two gentlemen came to meet me. One was the producer's brother, the other the porter from the Hotel Algonquin where I had booked rooms.

The hotel people greeted me as if I were a long-lost daughter who had at last come home. Oh, many of us know Mr. Case, the manager, and are not surprised, but why does the telephone girl smile so pleasantly, why does the elderly chambermaid talk to me as if she were my Nannie? And as for the waiter, no one in Europe could take a greater personal interest.

One of the Americans on the boat had said: "New York's awfully hot in August. If you're doing nothing over the week-end, why don't you come out to the country and stay with my cousin? I'm sure she'd be glad to have you. She's swell, and her two little kids are darlings. And you can get a drink there."

My nervous suggestion that perhaps the lady might not want a sudden uninvited guest met with ridicule. I *did* go to the country for the week-end (New York *was* hot) and the lady *was* swell, and we are still friends.

On the Monday morning I walked down Broadway, vulgar noisy greasy Broadway. I needed some stockings and there was what I still call a "dearie-shop" on a corner. (A "dearie-shop" is a place where the salesgirls call you "dearie".) A very pretty girl with a good manicure and lovely hair chewed gum and took endless trouble finding the right color and the right texture of hose for me. She smiled benignly and said: "Say, if you take three pairs you can get them for two-seventy-five. Say, Honey, you're from across the water, aren't you? Been here long?"

"Three days."

"Aw," she said tenderly, "I hope you like it here. Good luck."

I walked out of the shop with a light heart. I liked being Honey to a strange girl, I liked her taking fifteen minutes to sell me the right stockings, I liked her wishing me good luck, I liked her being pretty and not a cat. I had not yet been asked to "step on it" by a lift . . . no, an *elevator*-boy, and when he would do so, I now expected him to do it with a smile that would take the sting out of it.

That night I worried. I had come home. But that didn't make sense. I had left a perfectly good home in England, a good family, good friends. I ought to feel *that* was home. But it wasn't. *This* was. This was where I belonged. I knew it then, after three days.

When you belong to the oppressed, when you are a refugee, when you have failed in your vocation, when you have been poor as a stray dog in your native land, then you embrace Americanism with gratitude, and that is a good sort of love, too. But when you are young and a success in your work and comfortably off, and arrive as a visitor ready to criticize, then you embrace Americanism differently. Then you have fallen in love with a country. I had.

There are things to be remedied in America, things to change a little, wrongs to be righted. But they must be righted by the lovers, not the haters of the land, they must be worked for with tolerance and patience, and sometimes with shrewdness, as a woman works to improve the disposition of a person she loves.

ELISSA LANDI, Internationally known stage and screen actress, was born in Venice, Italy, and educated in such widely separated places as London, Vienna, Paris and Vancouver. She wrote several published novels while still in school and before beginning her stage career abroad. She came to the United States in 1930 and played many notable screen parts. She now devotes the major part of her time to writing successful novels and the care of her farm in upper New York State.

by Ludwig Bemelmans

I<small>T</small> <small>WOULD</small> <small>SOUND</small> foolish to say you loved a country because Majors here call their Adjutants "Charlie", wouldn't it? But that is one of my reasons for loving America. Perhaps I really mean that I like America because it's so different from any other place. You couldn't take your dog into the Army with you in Austria where I was born, for instance. But when I joined the United States Army in 1917 I told the Major that I had a dog, and the Major said to his Adjutant, "Say, Charlie, he has a dog—can we use a dog?" and Charlie hollered back, "It's all right with me", and the Major said, "All right son, bring your dog". The Adjutant had his legs on the Major's desk, and the Major told me how much he had enjoyed a trip down the Rhine, and that's one of the reasons I love America.

I was still new enough in this country to be surprised

at things being so different from what I expected. Of course, I knew about the Indians and the elevated railway by that time.

When I sailed from Rotterdam to America I bought two pistols and much ammunition to protect myself from the Indians. I'd been reading Fenimore Cooper, you see, to bone up on America. My other idea about the country was that the elevated railroad of New York ran over the housetops, adjusting itself to the height of the buildings like a roller coaster. By the time I got into the Army I knew better than that. But I still didn't speak English very well.

It's a wonder they let me into the Army with a German accent—they might have taken me for a spy or something but they thought the accent was funny. They used to yell, "Come on, Bemmy, do your stuff!", and then applaud when I said something as if I was a comedian giving a performance. Except the time I was on sentry duty in New Jersey and told the Colonel to "Advance and be recognized". I must have had trouble saying that word "recognized" because the Colonel stopped and said, "Good Heavens! Have the Germans got this far?"

Americans expect people to be human beings—and many Germans insist on their being machines. Take the matter of discipline, for instance. When I first joined the American Army I had the German idea of discipline. Many Germans are too subordinate. They are willing to be kicked as long as there is someone below to whom they can pass that kick. But I did not realize how different discipline under a Democracy was—so one night when I was appointed Wardmaster in the Hospital Ward of a camp in New York State, I turned off the lights at nine o'clock. The men shouted for me to turn them on again. I told them that the orders were "Lights out at Nine o'clock". "That's right", said one of them, "But it doesn't say we can't turn them on again!" I ran over to the barracks and got my Colt Forty-five and came back to the ward. I told them that the first time the light was turned on I would shoot. They howled with joy and turned the lights on. So I shot twice over their heads!

People came running. They took away my gun and brought me to the Colonel's headquarters. I told him how it happened—how discipline was the first requisite of an Army. The Colonel looked out of the window. "The basic function of a hospital, Private Bemelmans", he started to say, "is to cure men and not to shoot them". Then he laughed, and everybody laughed, and soon after that I was transferred to guard duty.

Certainly I learned a lot about Americans by being in the Army, but I have set my mind against speaking or thinking of nations in the mass—all Americans are such and such, all Germans are thus and so. That is unfair. People are much the same everywhere. I think if Americans fight a war they do it as they would repair a truck. It's a job, but they don't hate the people they fight with, like German soldiers. Tolerance isn't just a fine word in a speech, it's the way those doughboys in 1917 treated a young German-born recruit—let me talk about Germany, even speak German. I was truly thankful for all that and it made me more of an American than the citizenship papers I carried in my pocket.

I'm afraid I haven't got any Message for the world in this little article. I love Democracy because it means that here people can be let alone. I love America partly because it is possible to travel for enormous distances here without anyone even bothering to ask where you are going, or why you are going there. I love America because we can take criticism! In some countries you can't do anything but flatter them, they are most eager to have you see everything good, but when you say, "Yes, it is beautiful, but aren't there a great many flies?" they have no use for you. I wrote that I loved America for the wrong reasons! You see that I am not the person to go to for a Message or to advise naturalized citizens how to be good Americans.

Perhaps there *is* one small thing I would like to tell them. There are people who have made their money in America, lived here most of their lives, married, and raised an American family and wouldn't for the world go back to their native land. And yet they persist in boasting about its greatness, like one of my own fellow countrymen, for instance, who is always asking one to drink toasts to the "greatest nation in the world", by which he means, not his new country America, but his

former country, Germany. Everyone must understand
that a naturalized citizen must have some affection for
the country he came from, no one would mind if he
speaks of its rivers and forests or of his childhood, but
if he still thinks after living in America that his native
country is the greatest in the world I think he should go
back there and take his money and his ideas of greatness
and his toasts with him.

However, I think that most naturalized citizens are
even more aware of the privileges they enjoy in this
country than native-born Americans themselves. You're
not only so thankful to be in America, but you're also so
thankful not to be anywhere else. There have been times
when I have been traveling in other countries in recent
years when I had it brought home to me how wonderful
it is to be an American.

On my recent trip to Ecuador I saw one taxicab in
Quito which was named Adolfo Hitlero. And I met a
man who told me that they had definite information that
President Roosevelt had ordered the Sixth Avenue Elevated torn down to be made into munitions for England.
But, to tell you the truth, I'm afraid the chief thing I
thought about in South America was food! American
food! It made me feel more patriotic than anything else
ever has—except for one time. That was three years ago,
in Berchtesgaden, Germany. I had gone there to get an
interview with Hitler for an American newspaper. I had
an appointment to see him, but I had waited four days

and still he did not come. It had rained all the time and there is not very much to do in Berchtesgaden except drink Gluenwein, a hot toddy with cinnamon and cloves steeped in it, which seems very innocent and harmless, and isn't so at all. One afternoon my companion, a Tyrolean guide and I sat in the inn and we saw that something was about to happen.

The expected subject of my interview did not arrive but his voice did. There was a radio in the big room of the inn and all the townspeople gathered to listen to a speech and when it was concluded something impelled me—the Gluenwein it must have been—to rise to my feet and give an imitation of the speaker, with a cigar leaf stuck under my nose for a mustache. The next thing that I knew I found myself in the hands of the Political Police.

I realized that I had chosen an unfortunate spot for my imitation when I found myself escorted solemnly to a cell in the Munich prison. A small, pale fellow shared the cell with me. He told me that he had been in solitary confinement for six months. I was the first person he had spoken to in that time. He said, "I was the editor of a small paper. Up to now I have not been informed of the charges against me. I have no lawyer. I don't even know what has become of my wife and three children, but I am thankful to have someone to talk to . . ." He asked me why I was there and I told him the whole story of my regrettable fondness for imitations. He said, "You

174

won't be here long. An American citizen—how enviable, how fortunate for you! You will walk in the streets this evening, or tomorrow evening and hear the bells of the tramways and see people, and eat in a restaurant, and listen to the music playing . . ."

He gripped my shoulder with his hand and added, "but if anything should go wrong, and they lock you up alone as they have me, I will tell you what will help you. Somewhere in your cell you will find a place where a patch on the cement, a trick of the shadows—something will outline for you the face of someone you love—after a while it will be there for you strong and clear to help you when the trembling starts—when the terror comes . . ."

My American passport saved me from the consequences of the regrettable incident. But that was not the only reason, you see now, why, when I left that prison I was grateful and proud to be able to say, "Thank God —that I am an American!"

LUDWIG BEMELMANS was born in Meran, Tirol, in 1898. When he came to the United States in 1914 he worked as a busboy in a Chinese restaurant. Sometime later he was the proprietor of the Hapsburg, one of the finest restaurants in New York. For the past few years he has devoted all the time he could spare from his wife, and his daughter to writing and illustrating. The studio of Jascha Heifetz and the stage decor for Noah *stand to* his credit, as do articles and stories in all of the foremost magazines. His books include "My War With the United States", the story of his army career, "Life Class", of his triumphs and vicissitudes as a waiter, "Small Beer" the panorama of a Tyrolean village. "The Donkey Inside", the story of Bemelmans' trip to Ecuador, is his latest volume.